THE REALIST NOVEL
IN ENGLAND

Also by Ioan Williams

THE REALIST NOVEL
IN ENGLAND

A Study in Development

IOAN WILLIAMS

M

First published 1974 *by*
THE MACMILLAN PRESS LTD
London and Basingstoke
Associated companies in New York
Dublin Melbourne Johannesburg and Madras

SBN 333 17148 9

Printed in Great Britain by
THE BOWERING PRESS LIMITED
Plymouth

Contents

vi   *Contents*

I Marged, fy mam, ac
er cof am fy nhad

Acknowledgements

At various times I have benefited greatly from the comments and conversation of my friends and colleagues, and among these I must mention particularly Dr A. Pilkington of Jesus College, Oxford, Dr D. Lodge of the University of Birmingham, Dr R. Lass and Professor B. Bergonzi of the University of Warwick. I must also thank the staff of the University of Warwick Library for the help they gave me during the time when I was gathering material for this book.

Introduction
The Basis of Realism

The long reign of Queen Victoria has given us a term which is
not without usefulness in literary history. 'Victorian' con-
veniently describes the literature of a period which, though long
and varied, has a certain unity, distinct from Romantic literature on the one hand, and modern on the other. But students
of economic, social, and political history have long been conscious of the need to subdivide the Victorian period into shorter
phases, more clearly defined, and the same necessity holds true
for literature.[1] Like historians, we can discern, within the steady
development of poetry and fiction through the period from the
1830s to the end of the nineteenth century, different phases and
lines of development.

Where the novel is concerned, we may first be impressed by
the elements of continuity. English novelists of the mid-nineteenth century were highly aware of the achievement of their
eighteenth century predecessors, constantly looking back
towards them and positioning themselves within an already
long and distinguished tradition. Similarly, writers of the later
decades were very conscious of what they inherited from Austen
and Scott, Dickens, Thackeray and George Eliot, though they
also looked further afield to French and Russian novelists, whose
influence they felt with at least equal immediacy and force.
Even so, there are major differences and agreements which
clearly distinguished certain phases of the novel's history from

others, and most prominent among these is the great creative phase of mid-Victorian fiction, taking up the period from 1845 to 1880, when the English novel underwent a period of intense development, not only in the hands of a small number of major writers, but in those of many lesser figures who used it with originality and power. We may say of this mid-Victorian period that it achieved what Erich Heller has called, 'the possibility of culture', in a community of men 'living together and maybe fighting one another, in a state of tacit agreement on what the nature and meaning of human existence is.'[2] This agreement expressed itself with special energy and effectiveness in the contemporary novel, and when it broke up, no matter what elements of continuity remained, a well-defined phase of the novel's history was over.

When we think of this mid-Victorian fiction, the idea of Realism rises naturally to mind. In the first instance, we notice that contemporary novelists and critics were themselves steadily drawn to it, in spite of initial distaste and suspicion. Then, since the end of the Victorian period, although artists have increasingly attacked the idea that Reality is to be established in the world of conventional physical perception, we have come to associate mid-Victorian literature with a naive confidence that Reality consisted in the material and social world around them. There is no doubt that the mid-Victorian novel rested on a massive confidence as to what the nature of Reality actually was, and that although it could not be identified with matter itself, it certainly lay in the material world. The way in which novelists of this period present human character, moreover, also brings the idea of the Real into prominence – they argue that unless the individual accepts that Reality lies outside himself and reconciles himself to its pressure upon him, he can never build a firm basis for personal morality or happiness. Finally, the texture and scope of mid-Victorian novels settle the question. Their solidity and firmness, their humour and breadth of interest in the abundance and variety of human character, and their unprecedented physical, social, and psychological detail, make the term Realist especially appropriate.

Realism is a notoriously slippery term, but the confusion it engenders generally arises from the fact that it is separated too far from the very positive and easily distinguishable factors which motivated its original invention and application. By now, of course, it is too late to reverse the process – from the original function of describing the fiction which first attempted to represent Reality in nineteenth century England, France and Germany, it will continue to be used to describe fiction which anticipates the characteristics of this literature, or, independent of chronology, to describe novels which embody other, generally 'truer' concepts of the real than that dominant in the mid-nineteenth century.

The origin of the term Realism, however, and the origin of the Realist fiction we are concerned with, both take us back to the eighteenth century, to the moment when artists and intellectuals in Europe abandoned the idea that art should show truth to nature and started to think in terms of using it to establish the nature of truth – finding truth within experience rather than making experience conform to some authoritative and arbitrary pattern derived from philosophy or theology. At this point art took on a new status and a new function, and although it has developed through successive generations as the idea of Reality itself has changed, it has rested on this fundamental assumption and developed along lines laid down at this time.

We are actually concerned here with two things – the abstract idea of Realism as a certain relationship between Reality and literature; and the concrete manifestations of this abstract idea, which necessarily took on a form showing the influence of ideas and attitudes which accompanied it historically, and developed along with these ideas and attitudes. So we must also trace the characteristic ideas of Realist fiction, which began to emerge when Romantic artists reacted against eighteenth century materialism and Idealism, and their own experience of aliena-

tion and disorientation that came with increasing self-consciousness.

The most important of these ideas was the organic conception
of experience, through which the artist unified disparate elements and brought together his self-perception with his perception of the material world. Associated with this conception
came new ideas about the imagination, or reason (as distinct
from understanding), faculties innate in man, allied to unreflecting consciousness, by which he apprehended total Reality
as an undivided whole and himself as one of its parts. Increasingly, too, at this time, the artist concerned himself with past
states or golden times, with innocence and primitive unconsciousness; with nature, or the poet's response to it; and with
ideal love, defined by Shelley as 'that powerful attraction
towards all we conceive or fear or hope beyond ourselves when
we find within our own thoughts the chasm of an insufficient
void . . . the bond and the sanction which connects not only
man with man, but with everything that exists.'[3]

And these organic views of life necessarily came together
with the new way of thinking about art, to produce the concept of the work of art as an organism, conveying its 'meaning'
(a reflection of Reality), through texture and structure. As the
product of imagination, it embodied the principles and proportions implicit in experience itself. Consequently it claimed to be
free of externally derived criteria, to shake off intrusive moral
questions, and to express its meaning through structure. As
such it demanded a new criticism, which in Germany was quick
to develop but in England came only slowly, lagging years
behind.[4] In the interval English criticism was unable to adjust
to the new forms of art, and went on applying mechanistic
criteria, based on the assumption that all works of art should
comply with externally derived rules.

Nineteenth century Realist fiction in England is a form of
Romantic art, but it differs from Romantic art itself in throwing
emphasis on the importance of reproducing the external conditions of life and the material laws. It emerges from Romanticism

by a process of natural development of central Romantic ideas
under the influence of new social forces. Organic conceptions
are central to mid-Victorian literature, though more difficult
to express in representations of everyday social life. Like their
predecessors, Victorian artists were also fundamentally sentimentalists, though they attacked subjectivism. They saw the
simple emotional needs of mankind as the only medium of self-
fulfilment, and they stressed the sympathetic emotions as the
basis of morality, which was specially important to them
because it was the factor which allowed the individual to integrate emotional and spiritual elements of his own nature, and
conform to social laws. Like the Romantic poets, they were
basically suspicious of the analytical intellect, but they accepted
it as a necessary qualification of the emotions, and a condition
of proper understanding of the individual's place in the universe. Their aesthetic ideas were also fundamentally Romantic,
though they tended to replace the imagination by the sympathetic emotion of the artist, which enables him to detect the
spiritual elements in human character.

The most fundamental common element in the work of the
mid-Victorian novelist, however, is probably the idea that
human life, whatever the particular conditions, may ultimately
be seen as unified and coherent. And it was on this point that
English writers differed from their French counterparts. French
Realists accepted the aesthetic implications of organicism, but
rejected the moral and social. Realism in France had emerged
as an anti-Romantic mode, opposed to the idealisation and
heightening of experience which was felt to be characteristic
of French Romantic literature. In reaction, the French Realists
emphasised man's subjection to material laws and tended to
represent morbid states of mind and repressive aspects of social
experience. These tendencies, increasing Victorian suspicion of
the French as unstable and amoral, gave the idea of Realism
derogatory associations in England, which it took some decades
to shake off. It also meant that literary debate in England was
likely to take the term Realism as referring only to the repre-

sentation of material conditions and laws, or unpleasant aspects of experience, leaving a sense that some other term was needed to describe the mode of art which expressed all Reality. Consequently, although no single mid-Victorian writer would have claimed it, the term Idealism remained current; and critics tended to speak of contemporary art as requiring the reconciliation of the two contrasting modes.

Reconciliation of disparate or contrasting elements of experience is the fundamental aim of Victorian novelists. This has moral and aesthetic implications – beauty and truth are attained by the same means. In addition, novelists of this period believed that their aim was to be achieved by understanding and representing the proportions and relations of different aspects of individual and social experience, and the material conditions of life. These ideas, together with the moral and philosophical value placed on the process of chastening and adjustment which ended in social integration and marriage, made up a firm and flexible framework within which they worked.

It is the purpose of this book to trace the way in which this framework was put together, and to follow the processes by which the attitudes and aims dependent on them also developed. This can only be done by moving outside the novel itself, so as to keep in mind the novel's dependence on patterns of action, conceptions of character and moral values which derive from literary tradition and contemporary culture. This is not a study of influence or relationships between individual authors, but rather of shared elements of experience. It rests on the assumption that the development of literary form is inextricably related to the development of sensibility or culture. Consequently it attempts to identify the elements common to all writers, the material from which they form their own thoughts under the influence of personal factors, and also to record the way in which this common material was given new shape by individual writers.

One final word; the particular authors treated in the following chapters selected themselves on the grounds either of their typicality at a given moment, or the originality with which they moulded contemporary ideas and forms of perception. Taken to its logical conclusion in terms of length and comprehensiveness the method of study would enable the reader to bring in not only major figures like Charlotte or Emily Brontë or Anthony Trollope, but lesser figures, like Wilkie Collins, Charles Reade or Charles Lever. But if the book has a value as it stands, it may safely be left to the reader to establish its relationship with other novelists, or with the poets, dramatists and essayists of the period. Its highest claim is to be a sketch from nature, which brings into outline the principle lines of its subject.

Part I

1 The English Novel in the Romantic Period

The rise of the novel to dominance over other literary forms in the mid-nineteenth century was a sudden event. The expansion of range and technical development which accompanied the rise can be located quite clearly in the late 1840s, when Dickens and Thackeray were beginning to produce their mature work and when so many younger novelists were beginning to write almost at one moment. The fact that this development was so much a general one, and that Dickens and Thackeray were not writing in relative isolation, as earlier Richardson and Fielding or Scott and Austen had done, requires explanation. The novel's actual development in mid-Victorian England is so closely connected with the assimilation of Romantic ideas that we are compelled to ask why it had not undergone a similar expansion before, at the time when other literary forms were being transformed, in the period from 1790 to 1825.

In fact the English novel in the later part of the eighteenth century was committed to a kind of conservatism which prevented the assimilation of the leading ideas of Romantic artists. In the years following the great development which the novel had undergone in the hands of Richardson and Fielding, its characteristic features, as one critic has put it, were its popularity as a form of entertainment and its inferiority as a form of art.[1] Richardson's fundamental innovation (which in some respects Fielding had set himself against) was the development of a form which embodied the tension between conscious and subconscious motivating factors. This was widely appreciated in France as giving a whole new emphasis to individual experience. So Richardson's achievement was furthered by Rousseau, Diderot and Laclos, who adapted his method to investigate the area of conflict between individual experience and superimposed moral and social law. In the hands of these writers the novel moved steadily forward, claiming new importance as the proper medium for the investigation of the modern consciousness – where rationalistic, sentimental and traditional pressures came into conflict and had to be resolved.

In England this could not happen. The novel was very soon felt to be a potentially subversive form and was forced to conform to traditional aesthetic and moral requirements. The example of Fielding in this respect was not entirely beneficial because his authority was used to turn the novel back towards satirical functions and make it serve the purposes of 'commonsense' philosophy. So when it became possible for new kinds of poetry to be written, illustrating fundamentally new aesthetic and moral ideas, the novel was left on an essentially conservative basis – a strong one, because it drew strength from tradition, but unsuitable as the starting point of consistent development.

According to the view dominant throughout the eighteenth century, fiction was the result of an intellectually primitive attempt to explain the world in terms of fancy, crudely combining inadequate materials.[2] Fiction originated and was powerful in the primitive stages of civilisation and was naturally expected to lose its power as civilisation proceeded. It would appeal to the mind of the child, but not to the mature man. Indeed, as Johnson said, the appeal of the contemporary novel was to the young, the ignorant, and the idle, rather than to those who might benefit from it, sifting the good from the evil.[3] Consequently it was dangerous, distracting from serious study and preventing the individual from attaining intellectual maturity. Worse still, it could pervert the judgement by giving false impressions and so affect the moral view, which depended on the true understanding of objects and actions. In women and young girls there could be a further effect. Novels were capable of over stimulating the imagination and of producing desires which reality could not satisfy. They could also, by exciting the fancy, produce sexual stimulus in the female. So it is not surprising that moralists, philosophers and even learned physicians, inveighed against the whole business of novel writing and novel reading – especially after the development of the circulating library system, which put them in the hands of those they affected most easily. From reading *Clarissa*, there were those pessimistic enough to argue, it was but a step to running away with the footman.

The writers of sentimental romance and Gothic novel defended themselves from this kind of attack by arguing that they were educating the sensibility of their readers and so affecting the formation of the moral sense and the judgement by the back door. These ladies defended fiction as a way of supporting the social, religious and cultural establishment by encouraging benevolence and sensitivity towards other people. Moralists countered this specious plea by saying that the reader of such fiction, seduced by the vision of enchanting distress, would have little time for distress in rags and homespun. Mrs Barbauld put it firmly:

> The objects of pity in romance are as different from those in real life as our husbandmen from the shepherds of Arcadia; and a girl who will sit weeping the whole night at the delicate distresses of a lady Charlotte or a lady Julia, shall be little moved at the complaint of her neighbour, who, in homely phrase and vulgar accent, laments to her that she is not able to get bread for her family.[4]

To the modern reader the most interesting thing about these arguments pro and con is that they reflect the same basic assumption – that fiction has no essential function, but exists only to fulfil some incidental purpose, good or bad.

The one sure refuge for the beleaguered novelist in the eighteenth century lay in the direction pointed by Cervantes and Fielding – the novel could be made to serve the purpose of satire, or criticism. It could be made a method of correcting judgement and mocking departures from orthodoxy in morals or mental balance. The authority of this view was supported by the example of the French comic novelists and satirists of the seventeenth century, Scarron and Furetière; and its weight is brought out in a consideration of the many novels in English which depend on the idea of the Quixotic confrontation between the deluded individual and reality. Reaction to the excesses of the sentimental novel and drama strengthened this aspect of contemporary attitudes to fiction as the century grew older, and in the later years, after the French Revolution and the Napoleonic wars, when English society in general contracted its ideas and political conservatism, reinforced an already powerful movement against the forces which seemed to undermine increasingly strict codes of morality and social behaviour, the novel actually came to seem, on the basis of its critical function, for the first time a completely respectable literary form.

During the period of the revolutionary and Napoleonic wars English society as a whole, subject to the deeper social and cultural trends most positively and sensitively recognised by the Romantic poets, moved away from the loose morality associated with the aristocracy towards a code which placed greater emphasis on the moral bearing of the individual. This development was associated with the growth of political reaction, so that the new moral awareness was used for political ends. As we see from the pages of the *Anti-Jacobin*, sentimentalism, Wertherism and the dramas of Kotzebue were lumped together with religious dissent and political liberalism, and collectively condemned as tending to moral laxity. The tone of discussions in genteel society at this time is illustrated, though perhaps in extreme form, by the memoirs of Baron Cockburn, a young man during the war years, whose parents were slightly older than Austen and Scott. Throughout the war, Cockburn reports,

it was impossible to hold a public meeting on a political subject
in Edinburgh. Society was obsessed with the horrors of the
Revolution and the obsession was manipulated for political
purposes. 'Grown up people talked at this time of nothing but
the French Revolution and its supposed consequences . . . If the
ladies and gentlemen who formed the society of my father's
house believed all they said about the horrors of French blood-
shed, and of the anxiety of people here to imitate them, they
must have been wretched indeed. Their talk sent me to bed shud-
dering.'[5] When reaction against this exaggerated fear did come,
it took the form of the adaptation of the rationalist methods
of eighteenth century French *philosophes* to serve the interests
of established parties in England. The organs of the new movement, the *Edinburgh* and *Quarterly*, continued the attack on
Romantic literature and on subjectivism and sentimentalism in
general. The predominant literary conservatism lasted well into
the third decade of the new century, reinforced by public
reaction to the challenge embodied in the poetry of Byron and
Shelley. Even the Tory Scott sometimes found himself caught up
in the conflagrations which lit up the pages of periodicals like
the *New Monthly Magazine*, where, in 1821, Meg Merilees was
bundled together with Lara and Cain:

> The fashionable notion now is, that in a work of true genius,
> everything must be made subordinate to passion – no matter
> how unnatural or presumptuous a tone it may assume; and
> accordingly our recent literature has teemed with impassioned
> railers against the decencies of life – impassioned marauders
> by sea and land – impassioned voluptuaries – impassioned
> renegades – impassioned striplings – impassioned hags – all of
> them venting furious sublimity.[6]

By 1821 this attitude was no longer so widely predominant
as it had been, but in the years when Austen and Scott were
thinking most seriously about the nature of fiction it had the
irresistible force of political necessity and social convention. The
result, around the turn of the century, was a spate of novels

which burlesqued the sentimental romance and the political attitudes associated with it. Jane Austen's *Love and Freindship* and *Northanger Abbey* are but the most interesting of a list which includes Isaac D'Israeli's *Vaurien* (1797), Sarah Greene's *Romance Readers and Romance Writers* (1810) and Edmund Barrett's *The Heroine* (1813). At the same time the conservative arguments strong throughout the second half of the century were refurbished by petty critic-moralists, who claimed to speak for sense and morality and who would suffer no fiction at all, although sanctified by wit, humour or passion. To people like the Reverend Mangin all fiction was pernicious, but the fiction of the previous half-century disastrous. Before his pious hopes for the future regeneration of the country, literary and intellectual distinctions vanished:

> The time, I trust, is to come, when the virtuous, the religious, the witty and the learned, will wonder equally at the profligacy and the weakness of us their forefathers; and will consign our *novels* to dust and darkness, as we have done by the monstrous effusions of Behn, and Etheridge, and Suckling; and when *Tom Jones* and *Roderick Random*, and Mr. Cumberland's *Henry*, and *The Sorrows of Werter*, and *Anna St. Ives*, and all the myriads which resemble them, will either not be found at all, or only in the cabinets of the curious and the reprobate.[7]

Few readers, one presumes, can have wholeheartedly accepted the flat platitudes masquerading as commentary in Rev Mangin's *Essay on Light Reading, As it may be supposed to influence Moral Conduct and Literary Taste*, but it is a typical example of the arguments behind the general tendency to depreciate novels against which the narrator of *Northanger Abbey* vigorously declaims. The contemporary novelist, in fact, was firmly fixed in the current of which Mangin's remarks form the froth, even if she were an independent and advanced thinker in other respects. Maria Edgeworth, for example, was something of a practical philosopher and educationalist.

Through her father she was an associate of Thomas Day; she travelled in France and owed a good deal to the ideas of the *philosophes*. Her *Castle Rackrent* is a highly original work of fiction and has a special interest as one of the links between Enlightenment rationalism and the wider, more humane vision embodied in the novels of Walter Scott. But Edgeworth's first venture into fiction shows the extent to which even she was deeply affected by the contemporary tendency to identify common sense and virtue and to make the novel subservient to them. *The Letters of Julia and Caroline* (1796) is typical of its period. It presents a contrasting pair of young women, one of whom is sensible and acts on the principles of rational virtue while the other illustrates the evils of sentimentalism. The series of letters begins with one from the aptly named Julia to her orthodox friend:

> In vain, dear Caroline, you urge me to *think*, I profess only to *feel*.
>
> *Reflect upon my feelings!* analyze my notions of happiness! explain to you my system! – My system! But I have no system: that is the very difference between us. My notions of happiness cannot be resolved into a simple, fixed, principle. Nor dare I even attempt to analyse them, the subtle essence would escape in the process . . .[8]

In the late eighteenth century there was only one possible end for a young person who gave herself to ideas such as these and Edgeworth's Julia reaches it quickly. She marries against reason, repents, elopes with a lover and abandons her daughter, who is cared for by Caroline. Later Julia returns, broken and penitent, to take a last painful glimpse of a child who does not even recognise her, and creeps upstairs to die in the bedroom of a happy home founded firmly on the principles of rational virtue.

The likeness between Edgeworth's Julia and Jane Austen's Marianne, between Caroline and Elinor, is a reminder of the extent to which Jane Austen belonged within the culture of

her period. Though she came to modify her approach to romantic affection between *Sense and Sensibility* and the later *Persua-
sion*, in her very latest, unfinished, novel *Sanditon* she was still
attacking sentimentality and subjectivism as inimical to virtue
and sense. Similarly, Sir Walter Scott set himself against the
kind of self-consciousness which in Byron's case had proved its
capacity to undermine the basis of happiness and virtue. In both
cases this rejection of the subjective element of experience prevented them from reaching an understanding of the new ideas
currently being expressed in poetry, drama and pictorial art.

In retrospect it is impossible to regret this conservatism. It is
difficult to imagine that a greater receptivity to romantic ideas
in fiction would have had greatly beneficial results. In Germany
even though this was one of its most intense periods of activity,
Romantic fiction did not amount to anything for which the
Englishman might wish to exchange the novels of Austen and
Scott. In France greater freedom seems only to have led to an
earlier exploitation of the ideas suggested by Scott than was
possible in England. In the long run the conservative fiction of
these two great novelists came to be seen as more revolutionary
in its way than the poetry of Byron or Shelley. Jane Austen
might almost be said to have provided the basic format for the
later Realist novel. In *Emma* she produced a novel which has
the authority of natural history. She presents, for the first time,
individual and social experience within a sharply realised social
and geographical context. She could have claimed, in a sense, to
have reconciled the achievement of Fielding and Richardson and
made possible a whole new kind of development in the English
novel. Walter Scott's contribution was more dramatic and more
quickly appreciated. He was the first to describe the forces at
work in human society as a whole and to show the individual
as the focal point of historical, economic and cultural forces
beyond his control. He was especially important because he also
managed to preserve his confidence in the possible harmony of
man's experience and in his essential dignity. The effect of his
work was to further the understanding of man's place in a

material universe and at the same time to spread democratic and philanthropic sentiment.

Consequently Austen and Scott must be understood to have contributed enormously to the development of the Realist novel of the mid-nineteenth century. Their conservatism was the condition of their achievement. It is also, however, the reason for the novel's failure to develop sooner or more consistently throughout the century's earlier decades. Though they remoulded the contemporary novel, they laid down no guidelines for its development in the immediate future. In the period which followed the decade when their most mature work was produced it was Wordsworth, Coleridge and Shelley who provided the stimulus and the guidance for those who sought to remould the experience of their generation.

2 The Novels of Jane Austen: Conservatism and Innovation

After a sustained reading of late eighteenth century English fiction, the novels of Jane Austen come like a breath of wind in the face. She is nothing short of revolutionary in the way she brings the novel down to the scale of actuality, capturing the freshness and vividness of dialogue that had previously belonged only in the theatre, and throwing the light of humour and satire over the areas of daily experience which impinge most sharply on our consciousness. In several ways she anticipates the leading features of later Realist fiction – what one critic describes as 'the classic form of the nineteenth century novel, a form that enables the artist to record both the flow of external events and the complexities of personal impressions'.[1] She is also highly aware of social and physical conditions limiting human freedom and, like her successors, attacks materialism. Like the Realist novelists, too she presents the assimilation of intellectual understanding and emotional sensitivity as the condition of moral well-being. In *Emma*, moreover, she foreshadows the typical methods and structural patterns of the later nineteenth century novel.

Modern critics concentrate on *Emma* because of its 'organic unity', through which the demands of the moral scheme are reconciled with 'a growing concern for the dynamics of character, for psychological exposition'.[2] But too great a concentration on *Emma* may obscure the fact that Jane Austen was actually unprepared to take the decisive step of integrating her moral statement with the objective narration of a specific event or experience. Her stance in *Emma*, as in the rest of her fiction, is that of one who believes that the immediate justification of the novel lies in its capacity as an instrument for examining moral problems. *Organic* unity, as distinct from the unity possessed by all successful works of art, refers to the complete integrity and independence of Romantic and post-Romantic fiction. Without aspiring to this, *Emma* approaches it more closely than Austen's other novels. But it actually falls short of the degree of integrity which is the aim of later novelists. The structure of *Emma*, though perfect of its kind, is not designed to represent the structure of experience as a whole.

The unity of *Emma* derives from the fact that the moral scheme, though strongly supported in other ways, is carried through the narrative and action of the learning process in the heroine. This represents a substantial advance in the history of English fiction and an essential step in the process by which the novel became capable of handling subjects and themes similar to those of Romantic poetry and drama. It must also be said that Austen's combination of internalised action and concrete social environment was an important example for later writers. Nevertheless, it is easy to exaggerate her originality, forgetting that her immediate successors felt no community of aim with her. In spite of appearances, the action of *Emma* does not really proceed according to the phases of a steady process of growth in the heroine. Jane Austen remains very much in charge, conducting the narrative from much the same angled view as in her earlier novels. The novel remains, in fact, within the tradition begun in English fiction with Charlotte Lennoxe's *Female Quixote* (1754), whose deluded heroine goes through a number of experiences which do not convince her that her view of life is wrong and eventually is intellectually convinced in debate with a Doctor of Theology. *Emma* is an infinitely better novel than its predecessor, and very much further

advanced historically. In *Emma* we do get an internalisation of
the central learning experience. The action of the novel is seen
to spring from the character and upbringing of the heroine, and
the learning process from pressures in Emma's society which
affected the formation of her character. What completes the
learning process in the heroine are the emotional responses she
finds herself making, which themselves suggest to her that she
is in the wrong. But though Emma is not convinced by debate,
the understanding she eventually reaches is in effect an intellectual understanding, very limited in its range and consequences. It consists in a readjustment or realignment of the
heroine's position within, what has been called a completely
unquestioned 'socio-moral reality.'[3] The understanding which
Emma – and the reader – achieves, moreover, is very limited in
its application. The novel contains no attempt to find a view
which would make life meaningful on its own terms, or to
democratise the values implicit in the heroine's situation. In
Emma both the problem and its solution are restricted to a
limited cultural and social group in which cultural, social and
moral values are inextricably connected.

The subject of *Emma* is the learning process which takes
place in the heroine. She develops from conceited complacency
through humiliation, discovery of her own limitations and
dependence on others, to a happy marriage and a more stable
moral bearing. The subject develops in three phases, which correspond to the novel's three volume divisions. In the first we
become aware of the potentially dangerous results for herself
and others which Emma's bearing may have. She draws Harriet
away from Robert Martin and attempts to involve her with Mr
Elton, only to discover in the darkness of the coach that is taking her from Randalls, that Elton's designs, and his character,
are other than she had conceived them. This experience teaches
the heroine very little. In her reflections on it she first accepts
her own fault and then minimises its effect on her conduct.
She sees herself as having been wrong in the degree rather than
the nature of her activity:

The first error and the worst lay at her door. It was foolish, it was wrong, to take so active a part in bringing any two people together. it was adventuring too far, assuming too much, making light of what ought to be simple. She was quite concerned, and ashamed and resolved to do such things no more.[4]

The later interview with Harriet, in which Emma has the un-enviable task of disillusioning her friend about Mr Elton's attitude to herself, proves more truly instructive. The sight of Harriet's distress, caused by herself, has considerable effect: 'she left her with every previous resolution confirmed of being humble and discreet, and repressing imagination all the rest of her life.'[5]

Emma has later to learn that there is far more wrong with her bearing than she realises at this stage, but the next phase of the novel does not contain any more serious shock for her. Volume I ends with the anticipation of Frank Churchill's visit to Highbury. The second volume is taken up with the action which follows the return of Jane Fairfax, with Frank's first visit, his departure and the postponement of the projected ball, and the introduction of Mrs Elton. For Emma, apart from the continuing education in social experience, the most important consequence of these events as they occur is the degree of self-knowledge she acquires as a result of her flirtation with Frank, culminating in the discovery that if she ever loved him it was not very seriously, and in the determination to make a match between him and Harriet. At the same time, during this phase of the novel's action she is preparing matter of deep humiliation for herself at a later stage.

It is in Volume III that Emma for the first time makes a substantial step towards self-awareness, as the result of her own increasing involvement in social situations in which she is not the centre and over which she loses control. The degree of her actual lack of power is only revealed to her later, but immediately after the incident at Box Hill, where she insults Miss

Bates, she is for the first time substantially humiliated. Knightley's reproach brings her abruptly to realise how seriously she has failed in the sensitivity and discernment of her position relative to others that is necessary to proper conduct. The capacity to learn even in this situation is mainly dependent on the as yet unrealised affection for Knightley, but it is also partly dependent on her gradual awareness that she has lost control of the situations in which she finds herself. The importance of this factor is brought out in Austen's description of the situation immediately after Knightley's forthright reproof:

> While they talked, they were advancing towards the carriage; it was ready; and, before she could speak again, he had handed her in. He had misinterpreted the feelings which had kept her face averted, and her tongue motionless. They were combined only of anger against herself, mortification, and deep concern. She had not been able to speak; and, on entering the carriage, sunk back a moment overcome – then reproaching herself for having taken no leave, making no acknowledgement, parting in apparent sullenness, she looked out with voice and hand eager to show a difference; but it was just too late. He had turned away, and the horses were in motion. She continued to look back, but in vain; and soon with what appeared unusual speed, they were half way down the hill, and every thing left far behind.[6]

Later on, after the deeper humiliation which follows Emma's realisation that she loves Knightley – which is intensified by virtue of the fact that it comes through Harriet, of all people – Emma learns the need for a new kind of control and management of situation. Out of consideration for Knightley, even though she fears that he wants to speak about Harriet, she prolongs their walk in the shrubbery:

> Emma could not bear to give him pain. He was wishing to confide in her – perhaps to consult her; – cost her what it would, she would listen. She might assist his resolution, or

reconcile him to it; she might give just praise to Harriet, or, by representing to him his own independence, relieve him from that state of indecision, which must be more intolerable than any alternative to such a mind as his. – They had reached the house.

'You are going in, I suppose,' said he.

'No' – replied Emma – quite confirmed by the depressed manner in which he still spoke – 'I should like to take another turn, Mr. Perry is not gone.'[7]

What she actually hears from Knightley is a charming recompense for her newly considerate behaviour.

Even after this happy revelation, the novel has a good way to go. Its latest sections are devoted to the inevitable business of tying up loose ends. Harriet must be settled, and Emma show that she has learnt to assess other characters as well as her own. Frank and Jane have to explain themselves, Mr Woodhouse to be persuaded to accept the idea of Emma's marriage. But this part of the novel actually has a good deal of importance in itself. A major element after Emma and Knightley have reached their understanding is his reading of the letter in which Frank explains his conduct. Through the device of making Knightley read and comment on the letter Austen is able to control our own reading of it. Our respect – tinged with amusement – for Emma's eminently solid lover qualifies the sympathy we would otherwise feel for the all too convincing explanations of the volatile Frank Churchill. In her use of this device we find evidence of Austen's continuing control and manipulation, not only of the story of Emma's development, but also of the complicated structure of character juxtaposition and debate which extends and subtilises the reader's process of learning.

The reader of *Emma* is actually being worked on throughout the novel, which educates him as thoroughly as Emma's experience educates her. This is done by combining several techniques. The flexibility which Austen maintains between report of Emma's state of mind and feeling and other elements of

narrative and comment, is the primary stylistic factor. We feel
its effects even when we are being informed with apparent
objectivity of the behaviour of the heroine. Jane Austen's
ironical method purports to give direct report and narrative, but
actually works so as to inform us about the moral content of
that behaviour, and at the same time amounts to an education
in the values which the novel exists to set forth. This is done
very clearly in the passage which describes Emma's approaches
towards Harriet Smith. From the beginning of the chapter we
sense that there is something wrong in Emma's conception of
a friend: 'Quick and decided in her ways,' Emma lost no time,
we are told, 'in inviting, encouraging and telling her to come
very often.' We notice the gradual build up of implication
through the three verbs. The same device is used a little further
on where three adjectives are employed to suggest that the
actual basis of Harriet's attractiveness lies in the extent to which
she can be managed and manipulated. Harriet, Austen's
narrator informs us, all the time maintaining a tone in which
it is very difficult to distinguish Emma's own thoughts from the
narrator's statements, 'had a sweet, docile, grateful disposition'.
It soon comes to seem as if Harriet is taking on something of
the status of an umbrella: 'As *a walking companion*' Emma
had very early foreseen how *useful* she might find her . . . and
a Harriet Smith, therefore, *one whom she could summon at any
time* to a walk would be a valuable addition to her *privileges*.'[8]

It is also important that the novel works primarily through
scenes of dialogue which are essentially social scenes, in which
we are directly aware of the behaviour and general bearing of
characters other than the heroine. In the nineteenth century
bildungsroman the proportion of emphasis given to the subsidiary characters at the expense of the central figure was a
continual problem, often resulting in his weakness or passivity.
Austen avoids this problem precisely because she does not pretend to internalise the action of the novel beyond a certain point
and is able to leave her subsidiary characters free and independent because she presents Emma herself in basically the same

way. This is greatly important to her because the moral design
of the novel is worked out not only in the heroine but also in
the society around her. We can see, to an extent which is
denied even to the heroine, that other characters have a direct
relation to the central moral debate. Harriet and Mrs Elton and
Jane Fairfax are obviously important in this way. The gradual
process of coming to see them for what they actually are is part
of Emma's education, but so is it part of ours, our awareness
of their relevance to the central moral issues predating hers
considerably. Other characters, like Mr Weston and Mr Woodhouse, and even Mr Knightley, none of whom Emma ever
explicitly judges according to her new lights at the end of the
novel, we see throughout in their bearing on the necessary combination of good nature, formal politeness and intellectual discernment. Beneath the surface of the action, partly realised by
Emma herself, we can also see a number of relationships, like-
nesses and contrasts, which encourage us to make comparisons
between characters – between for example, Emma and Frank on
the one hand and Jane and Knightley on the other – and consequently to fill out conclusions about the relationship between
temperament and circumstances in their effect on moral
bearing.

　Emma also contains a certain amount of explicit debate,
which greatly extends its area of reference. Emma herself
becomes conscious of one important issue. Her early attitudes
on the subject of gentility, for example, and her undiscerning
tendency to overvalue the merely formal aspects, are knocked
out of her by experience. Early in the novel, when she is
attempting to turn Harriet against the idea of marriage with
Robert Martin, she tends to set up Mr Elton as the perfect
gentleman: 'In one respect, perhaps, Mr Elton's manners are
superior to Mr Knightley's or Mr Weston's. They have more
gentleness. They might be more safely held up as a pattern.'[9]
She comes soon enough to regret this particular judgement, but
it is a long while before she can do Robert Martin justice and
concede that Harriet will be 'the luckiest creature in the world,

to have created so steady and persevering an affection in such a man'.[10]

Other conversations which Emma does not have occasion to reflect on later have a direct bearing on the debate concerning the qualifications of a gentleman. At the end of Volume I, for example, when Emma and Knightley discuss the pending visit of Frank Churchill to Highbury after a long absence, we are introduced directly to a difference in attitude between them on the subject of the relationship between superficial charm of manners and 'English delicacy towards the feelings of other people'.[11] Through this conversation we are instructed directly. The sounder statements of Knightley provide us with criteria of judgement which we are able to utilise immediately in assessing Frank, while the levity of the heroine on this subject prepares us to be keener judges of her lack of awareness of the relationship between manners and morals.

This conversation has a further element of great importance in the novel. Towards the end Knightley shows signs of irritation which perplex Emma herself and for which we have at the time no explanation. It is only our gradual awareness of his attitude to the heroine that enables us to explain the source of the irritation. At this stage we are inadequate to make a proper assessment of the reported action. We remain so until the very end of the novel, when the revelation of the secret engagement between Frank and Jane throws a completely new light on the whole action up to that point, bringing out an area of significance of which we, like Emma, had been unaware. *Emma* is, in fact, though it gives no outward signs of being so, something of a mystery novel and by virtue of this fact its readers are subjected to much the same process that the heroine herself has to go through – a compulsory and unexpected reassessment of characters and actions that have either been taken in a different way or simply ignored until the revelation is made.

As generations of critics have argued, *Emma* is perfectly unified. The balance Austen struck in this novel between internalisation of action, externally presented characters and situations, and elements of commentary and authoritative assessment and categorisation of behaviour, is completely successful as nothing else in her work is. Her originality is of the highest kind, in that she not only produces new material and new techniques, but also succeeds in synthesising them. The understanding at which Emma and the reader arrive is itself limited. It consists of readjustment, an emotional shock, followed by a process of intellectual readjustment to experience, but involves no question nor any attempt to validate the terms in which experience is categorised. Emma's discernment amounts to a new understanding of the relationship between fixed qualities, all of which she had been previously aware of, and all of which are brought from outside the novel's own boundaries, assumed alike by its personages and by the narrator.

In the first shock which follows Emma's discovery that she loves Mr Knightley herself she achieves clear understanding of her previous actions. Immediately she brings into effectiveness categories of moral assessment which we have seen in operation throughout. Explicitly they are categories of judgement:

> Her own conduct, as well as her own heart, was before her in the same few minutes. She saw it all with a clearness which had never blessed her before. How improperly she had been acting by Harriet! How inconsiderate, how indelicate, how irrational, how unfeeling, had been her conduct! What blindness, what madness, had led her on.[12]

Reflection increases the dreadful force of the revelation, but the nature of her reflections remains the same. Emma is shocked, humiliated and suddenly able to see her behaviour from a new point of view – very close to the one which Knightley has possessed throughout, and which he had shared with Austen's narrator:

> The rest of the day, the following night, were hardly enough for her thoughts – She was bewildered amidst the confusion of all that had rushed on her within the last few hours. Every

moment had brought a fresh surprise and every surprise must be matter of humiliation to her. – How to understand it all! How to understand the deceptions she had thus been practising on herself and living under! – The blunders, the blindness, of her own head and heart.

To understand, thoroughly understand her own heart was the first endeavour. . . . She saw that in persuading herself, in fancying, in acting to the contrary, she had been entirely under a delusion, totally ignorant of her own heart – and, in short, that she had never really cared for Frank Churchill at all!

This was the conclusion of the first series of reflections. This was the knowledge of herself, on the first question of inquiry, which she reached; and without being long in reaching it. – She was most sorrowfully indignant; ashamed of every sensation but the one revealed to her – her affection for Mr. Knightley. – Every other part of her mind was disgusting.[13]

It is interesting to compare these passages with the one Austen wrote much earlier to describe Elizabeth Bennett's sensations on reading the letter in which Darcy vindicates his own behaviour towards Jane and Wickham:

She grew absolutely ashamed of herself. Of neither Darcy nor Wickham could she think, without feeling that she had been blind, partial, prejudiced, absurd.

'How despicably have I acted!' She cried. – 'I, who have prided myself on my discernment! I, who have valued myself on my abilities! who have often disdained the generous candour of my sister, and gratified my vanity, in useless or blameable distrust. – How humiliating is this discovery! – Yet how just a humiliation! Had I been in love, I could not have been more wretchedly blind. But vanity, not love, has been my folly . . . I have courted prepossession and ignorance, and driven reason away, where either were concerned. Till this moment, I never knew myself.'[14]

Elizabeth and Emma are different, as are their circumstances and problems; but the way in which they solve them is basically similar. Shock, followed by humiliation, producing clear vision and intellectual understanding of the individual's relationship with a fixed and unquestioned actuality. In spite of her substantial advance in the internalisation of action, Austen took no step towards accepting that value itself can be established through internal individual experience, but instead brought the emotional sensitivity of the individual to serve as a qualifying factor in a system of judgement which was basically external and arbitrary.

Jane Austen consequently did not think of the novel's function as exploratory or self-determining, and in this historically conservative view lay the foundation of her actual success as a novelist. It is interesting, in this respect, to compare her with Goethe. The author of *Wilhelm Meister* brought to the novel much greater understanding of the pressures implicit in modern experience. Consequently his novel possessed a far more widely-reaching originality than she achieved, and acted, in the period immediately after its composition, as an on-going influence while her work was relatively ignored. But, as Roy Pascal has pointed out, the comparison is by no means entirely to Goethe's advantage:

> If we compare *Wilhelm Meister* with the novels of . . . Jane Austen, it is clear that it probes deeper into human fate and shapes situations and characters that were beyond the imagination of the English writer; at the same time it is, in a peculiar sense, far less mature as a work of art than such works as *Emma*, not only in the indefiniteness of its general shape, but also in the impression of many characters and events. This immaturity belongs to its whole nature. For while Jane Austen, like all the classical novelists, was concerned to show characters choosing between certain moral alternatives within an unquestioned socio-moral reality, the main task for Wilhelm Meister is to discover the validity of

this reality and of moral decision altogether. The novel is the story of this discovery.[15]

Goethe's understanding of the importance of internalising the action of his novel brought with it no understanding of the means of unifying the internal experience of his hero with the objective, totally external, portrayal of other characters. So *Wilhelm Meister*, astonishingly modern in some respects, seems in others far more reminiscent of eighteenth century fiction than *Emma*, and is seriously marred by artificiality, vagueness and frigidity of characterisation. Jane Austen succeeds exactly where Goethe fails, and by virtue of being a 'classical' novelist, reposing on the certainties of the eighteenth century world, is able to embody aspects of modern experience which had never been presented in the novel before, and which were to form the material of the later nineteenth century novel, though moulded under forces and influences of which she had no conception.

3 Inspiration and Inhibition in the Novels of Walter Scott

Walter Scott's fiction shows man more fully than he had been shown since Cervantes. He shows the major social and political forces at work on the individual. He shows how men are determined, their circumstances affected by forces beyond their control and their characters formed by the social and religious community in which they are brought up. Yet Scott's view of character is not in the final analysis deterministic. His enormous influence throughout the nineteenth century sprang from the fact that he offered, though not explicitly, a resolution of the conflict between determinist and idealist view of character. His novels abound with characters who are powerful in their effect on others and on the reader, characters who may become tragic through their inability to adjust to changing circumstances, but who are also heroic and sublime in their completeness. The most insistent note in Scott's presentation of history regards the ineffectiveness of heroism and the impossibility of human freedom. Yet in the web of history itself we find abundance of characters, often at the very lowest social level and stunted by education and circumstance, who seem in the last analysis completely self-fulfilled. The death of Evan Dhu, the defeat of Redgauntlet, the poverty of Edie Ochiltree or Meg Merilees, stand out in a world where heroic gestures are robbed of meaning in a way which suggests that human character itself remains heroic and sublime.

B*

The originality and power with which he presented this view of experience made Scott's fiction a major element throughout the century after his death. Yet even when his reputation was at its height he was being subjected to the most fundamental criticism. Nineteenth century admirers were disappointed, as Frederick Denison Maurice put it, at his entire unawareness of the spiritual dimension of experience, or as Carlyle more bluntly expressed it, his total failure to see below the surface.[1] Later critics, perhaps with a more objective appreciation of Scott's real depth of his vision, complain at the striking lack of structural coherence in his novels and repeat old charges about the inadequacy of his central characters. These two criticisms, in fact, are connected. The weakness of Scott's heroes and the mechanical and unconvincing plotting both result from his failure to internalise the action of his novels. More important, they are also inevitable, the necessary consequences of his peculiar kind of intellectual conservatism on which, in fact, his whole creative achievement was based.

Scott's persistent failures in structure and characterisation are clearly interdependent. Not all of his work is lacking in structural coherence – as a narrator of tales he is unsurpassed; and where there is no demand for him to connect external action with the representation of internal processes of development, his characterisation is unflawed. In the extended tale *The Two Drovers* (1827) for example, he works the same materials as in his novels, but produces a completely coherent and convincing fiction. Both the central characters are typical and clearly-marked individuals. Robin Oig and Harry Wakefield, Yorkshire cattle merchants, both represent what is best in the culture that has moulded them. Against all probability they develop a friendship which seems to thrive on the difference between them, but as circumstances develop those differences come to have the predictable and eventually tragic effect of bringing about a headlong collision. In his presentation of the drovers and his awareness of the factors which are of most significance in their story, Scott shows how much he must have

learned from the French Enlightenment novelists. Robin and
Harry travel together from the Highlands to the English cattle
mart. Before they set out an event of ill omen has awakened
Robin's superstition and caused him to leave his knife behind
in the keeping of a friend who is to set out later. Towards the
end of the journey the two drovers separate to seek pasture
for their cattle and find themselves in unconscious competition.
The Englishman's irritability, excited by what he unreasonably
feels is the Scot's sharp practice, is further increased by drink.
He is worked up to the point when he insists on fighting his
friend, and at this stage the difference in background begins
to have serious importance. To the Englishman, a skilled boxer
of yeoman blood, the fight with fists is a natural end to a
quarrel, which can be wiped out of memory as soon as one
antagonist has admitted defeat. To Robin Oig, the Highlander,
intensely conscious of his noble blood, the insult of a blow and
the fiasco of a boxing match is a terrible humiliation which
can only be wiped out with blood. Not having his knife to
hand in the first moment of humiliation, he returns the six
miles to collect it, walks back, enters the tavern and calls
Wakefield to his feet. What follows is related with economy
and drama:

'Harry Wakefield,' repeated the same ominous summons,
'stand up, if you be a man!'
There is something in the tone of deep and concentrated
passion which attracts attention and imposes awe, even by
the very sound. The guests shrank back on every side, and
gazed at the Highlander as he stood in the middle of them,
his brows bent and his features rigid with resolution.
'I will stand up with all my heart, Robin, my boy, but it
shall be to shake hands with you, and drink down all un-
kindness. It is not the fault of your heart, man, that you
don't know how to clench your hands.'
By this time he stood opposite to his antagonist; his open
and unsuspecting look strangely contrasted with the stern

purpose which gleamed wild, dark, and vindictive in the eyes
of the Highlander.

' 'Tis not thy fault man, that, not having the luck to be
an Englishman, thou canst not fight more than a school-
girl.'

'I *can* fight,' answered Robin Oig sternly, but calmly, 'and
you shall know it. You, Harry Wakefield, showed me today
how the Saxon churl fights – I show you now how the Highland dunniewassel fights.'

He seconded the word with the action, and plunged the
dagger, which he suddenly displayed, into the broad breast
of the English yeoman, with such fatal certainty and force
that the hilt made a hollow sound against the breast bone,
and the double-edged point split the very heart of his victim.
Harry Wakefield fell and expired with a single groan.[2]

What remains of the tale finely illustrates Scott's own
attitude to his characters. Robin is tried; the prosecution
attempts to excite national prejudice against the vengeful Scot,
but the summary of the presiding judge is a fine example of
enlightened understanding. The judge takes into account the
full degree of irritation which preceded the offence and fastens
on the period of time which had intervened between the insult
and the blow. He understands Robin's motive, and knows as
well as any Enlightenment historian or natural philosopher
that it derives from the society in which he has been brought
up, and eventually from the social conditions in the Highlands.
Yet he insists on the rights of the law and instructs the jury to
find Robin guilty :

I repeat that this unhappy man ought personally to be the
object of our pity than our abhorrence, for he failed in his
ignorance, and from mistaken notions of honour. But his
crime is not the less that of murder, gentlemen, and in your
high and important office, it is your duty so to find. Englishmen have their angry passions as well as Scots; and should
this man's action remain unpunished, you may unsheath,

under various pretences, a thousand daggers betwixt the Land's end and the Orkneys.[3]

The story ends, not even with the judge's compassionate reasoning, however, but with the words of the hero himself. As always in Scott, it is the individual who claims priority of place before the statement of principle. The bystanders revile him for attacking an unarmed man. His reply may not result from the author's own sense of the irony in the law's savage punishment, but it certainly leaves the reader free to form his own conclusion. And it leaves Robin free, too, deriving dignity from the fact that he accepted his execution even before he struck the blow:

> He met his fate with great firmness, and acknowledged the justice of the sentence. But he replied indignantly to the observations of those who accused him of attacking an un-armed man. 'I give a life for the life I took,' he said, 'and what can I do more?'[4]

The level of effectiveness which Scott attained in *The Two Drovers* was frequently reached in the Waverley novels as a whole but never sustained throughout a single novel. The short tale had its coherence. Within the bounds of a single incident he could select and expand through character sketches, background description and narration, dialogue and subordinate events. But the tale offered no basis for expansion of subject-matter beyond a certain point, soon reached. Consequently Scott needed to discover some technique and principle of construction which would allow his larger fictions to sustain a whole view of life. In effect he borrowed most in this respect from those who influenced him most in other ways, and turned to Shakespeare and Cervantes. They taught him to see aspects of man's life unobserved by eighteenth century writers. He learnt from them to see man as a social and a political animal and at the same time to take a general view of his nature and condition which could only be expressed through some system of significant juxtaposition and contrast such as he found in the History Plays and in *Don Quixote*. Scott had also, however, a purpose of his own, which obliged him to modify the basic romance pattern he took from Renaissance fiction and drama. In the first place he was concerned to make his novels serve something of the function of a guide book, incorporating geographical and social description. In the second, he wanted to convey the historically new conception of value and meaning residing in individual experience. To serve these ends he adapted the picaresque form as he took it from Le Sage and Smollett, and strengthened the psychological dimension which even with Fielding it was only just beginning to acquire. Further considerations, as Alexander Welsh has pointed out, obliged him to make his picaresque hero more passive than ever before. Only 'a nearly completely passive hero' could serve the Burkean function of showing that a member of society surrenders the right to action on his own behalf in exchange for protection, stability and the economic and cultural rewards depending on them.[5]

In essentials, Scott's first novel is typical of all his important fiction. *Waverley* presents the adventures of a central character who gets caught up in a social and political revolution. In following these adventures we learn about the disturbed society in which he finds himself and are instructed as to its social and historical causes. During this process we assimilate a moral view which suggests that the conditions of life are harsh, that sublimity, heroism and romance are attained only at the cost of peace of mind or life itself, and that the qualities which make life endurable or desirable for the individual are essentially domestic and mundane. At the same time, during an action in which personal and historical factors are intertwined, the central character undergoes moral and psychological development which reinforces the values implied by the 'historical' events. The moral tendency of the whole novel is to assert that value and meaning, in so far as they are attainable, reside in the emotional and cultural fulfilment of the individual which can only be achieved by adaptation to historical circumstances.

The background to the action of *Waverley* is the 1745 rebellion on behalf of the Stuarts, followed by the Jacobite invasion of England, its defeat, and the opening of the Scottish Highlands. The central action itself, however, springs from the movements of the youthful Edward Waverley, the representative of an English Jacobite family, who travels to Scotland to join a regiment of dragoons. Visiting family friends and travelling as a sightseer in the Highlands, he is involved in a mesh of misunderstanding and political intrigue which leads to his resignation from his regiment and his decision to take arms on behalf of Prince Charles Edward. The action ends when he is re-established in England, reconciled to the Hanoverian establishment and safely married.

Waverley begins with an account of Edward's education and its effect on his character, showing how it produced a habit of imaginative self-indulgence which prohibited rational self-control. Lacking any guiding principle, Waverley is left to indulge his imagination in a course of desultory reading which distracts his mind and weakens his will and judgement. Scott says of his hero in early manhood that 'he might be considered as ignorant, since he knew little of what adds dignity to man, and qualifies him to support and adorn an elevated situation in life'.[6] In the first place he is shown to lack the qualities necessary to the professional soldier. The narrator informs us: 'the vague and unsatisfactory course of reading which he had pursued, working upon a temper naturally retired and abstracted, had given him that wavering and unsettled habit of mind which is most adverse to study and riveted attention'.[7] This instability of character makes Waverley liable to momentary impulses, leaves him open to influence from any source and prevents him from following a steady course. So, after curiosity has drawn him to the Highlands, he is very easily kept there until his reputation is compromised. A rare exercise of will determines him to go southwards again, in order to clear his name, but he falls into the hands of the Hanoverian authorities, is rescued by people he does not know, returned to the Highlands, and packed off to the Pretender's court in Edinburgh where he becomes his own agent once again.

In the Pretender's army, at the battle of Preston, Waverley encounters the first experience which shocks him out of passivity. The death of Sergeant Houghton, son of his uncle's tenant, makes him realise his failure to maintain due responsibility as a military and social leader: '. . . the repeated expostulation of Houghton – "Ah, squire, why did you leave us?" rang like a knell in his ears.'[8]

> 'Yes', he said, 'I have indeed acted towards you with thoughtless cruelty. I brought you from your paternal fields, and the protection of a generous and kind landlord, and when I had subjected you to all the rigour of military discipline I shunned to bear my own share of the burden, and wandered from the duties I had undertaken, leaving alike those whom it was my business to protect and my own reputation, to suffer under the artifices of villany. O indolence and indecision of mind! if not in yourselves vices, to how much exquisite misery and mischief do you frequently prepare the way!'[9]

This process of education is continued during Waverley's service with the Pretender's army, as he learns about the sordid personal motives that contribute to the commitment of those around him. The decisive influence, however, belongs to Colonel Talbot, his uncle's friend, who has come to Scotland in search of him.

Waverley saves Talbot on the battlefield and is responsible for his safe-keeping as a prisoner of war. In the close contact which ensues he becomes aware of a concept of honour and loyalty very different from the unthinking Highland code. Talbot's bearing is that of a civilised man of the world who understands the dependence of all he values most on Hanoverian stability and personal discipline. Shaken by the discovery that Talbot has left his wife in ill-health to come to Scotland and is now forced to bear the news of her miscarriage and serious illness in captivity, Waverley proposes escape. Talbot reproves him, giving the younger man an example in integrity and steadfastness which he cannot ignore:

'I only did my duty', answered Colonel Talbot calmly, 'and I do not, ought not, to regret it. If the path of gratitude and honour were always smooth and easy, there would be little merit in following it; but it moves often in contradiction to our interest and passions, and sometimes to our better affections. These are the trials of life, and this, though not the least bitter', (the tears came unbidden to his eyes) 'is not the first which it has been my fate to encounter . . .'[10]

Waverley's experience gives him a width of understanding and sympathy which is beyond the English soldier, but Talbot represents the model on which he eventually forms himself.

The process of education takes a good deal of time. Though Waverley becomes more and more aware that his lack of self-knowledge has led him to isolate himself from all he really values in life, it is only after his physical separation from the Jacobite army that he really comes to understand himself. In long periods of enforced solitude he has the opportunity to look back over the recent past and come to grips with his own character and situation:

– and it was in many a winter walk by the shores of Ullswater, that he acquired a more complete mastery of a spirit tamed by adversity than his former experience had given him; and that he felt himself entitled to say firmly, though perhaps with a sigh, that the romance of his life was ended, and that its real history had now commenced.[11]

Finally, on his return to the devastated home of Baron Bradwardine, he sees the cost in pointless destruction and waste of the romantic adventure in which he has been engaged. Approaching the village which in a short time he had grown to love, he reflects on how much he has learnt in the few short months since he had left Waverley Honour:

Now how changed, how saddened, yet how elevated, was his character, within the course of a very few months! Danger and misfortune are rapid, though severe teachers. 'A sadder and a wiser man,' he felt, in internal confidence and mental dignity – a compensation for the gay dreams which, in his case, had so rapidly dissolved.[12]

Waverley's intellectual and moral development proceeds partly through his emotional development. Immature and romantic, he falls in love with Flora MacIvor; 'sadder and wiser', he learns to appreciate the more subdued qualities of Rose Bradwardine. Scott takes care that we should associate the personal qualities of the two girls with wider features. Rose is introduced to us partly through the environment she has adapted to her own tastes and restrained amusements. Waverley visits her apartment at the top of a tower, looking out over a projecting gallery which is 'crowded with flowers of different kinds' on to a 'most beautiful prospect', combining variety, picturesque beauty and the signs of cultivation and order. Flora, on the other hand, entertains her visitor in a wild and savage scene, whose beauty 'was of a stern and command-ing cast, as if in the act of expanding into grandeur'.[13]

The difference between the two girls is further marked by their taste in music. The Baron's aptly named daughter com-bined sensitivity with naturalness. The narrator comments:

It was perhaps owing to this sensibility to poetry, and power of combining expression with those of the musical notes, that her singing gave more pleasure to all the unlearned in music and even to many of the learned, than could have been com-municated by a much finer voice and more brilliant execu-tion, unguided by the same delicacy of feeling.[14]

Flora produces a wild and peculiar tone which harmonises with the sound of the waterfall and the evening breeze, and its effect on Waverley is to increase to the point of distress his confusion of feelings:

. . . the wild feelings of romantic delight with which he heard the first few notes she drew from her instrument amounted almost to a sense of pain. He would not for worlds have quitted his place by her side; yet he almost longed for solitude, that he might decipher and examine at leisure the complication of emotions which now agitated his bosom.[15]

Gradually, with her help, the hero realises that his love for Flora is shallowly based, and at the same time his affections begin to turn towards Rose. Eventually he comes to love her, not with the excitement of feelings awakened by Flora, but as a fitting companion for his newly discovered and thoroughly chastened self. Their marriage completes both aspects of the hero's development and the novel's action, it ends with the restoration of a modified form of stable society in Scotland and with Waverley's attainment of stability of character – two things, it is implied, which must be related in the modern world.

The conception of *Waverley* was profoundly original, and its construction extremely ingenious. Each part of the novel has its own thematic value and relates to other aspects so as to make a completely integrated moral statement. Yet at the same time *Waverley* is a very unsatisfactory novel, completely lacking the dramatic integration of theme and action that is one of the main requirements of post-Romantic criticism. It lacks proportion and authority. The focus shifts from Waverley's experience to historical commentary or character analysis in a way that suggests a lack of any stable purpose in the narrator. The novel is supposed to focus on the external adventures of the hero because they have internal significance. In fact, the selection and order of events within the novel is often governed more by convenience of plot. When Waverley leaves the Highlands, is captured and rescued, kept prisoner, in ignorance of the identity of his captors, and finally bundled off to Edinburgh, we realise that Scott is prepared to sacrifice our interest in the moral development of the hero for momentary effect. Nothing which happens here is misplaced in terms of plot. We later learn that Waverley's rescuer is Donald Bean Lane, instigated by Rose, and that the mysterious hut he is kept in is the hovel where the Baron later finds refuge with old Janet, Davie

Gellatley's mother. The problem lies in the fact that we become aware that Scott himself fails to take seriously what is supposed to be the novel's central structural principle.

This is apparent in other ways. Scott makes no attempt to alter the presentation of Waverley's experience in spite of the changes in his character and point of view. In fact he fails to develop any method of treating Waverley's internal experience convincingly or of integrating it with external action. At one of the most important moments in Waverley's adventures, when he is confronted by Flora at the Prince's court and shocked by her indifference, Scott totally avoids the task of realising for his readers his hero's actual experience. When the Prince takes Edward aside for a moment, to allow him to recover, the narrator breaks in with a mock-heroic simile which is calculated to reduce our serious interest to a minimum:

> If, my dear reader, thou hast ever happened to take post horses at —— , or at —— (one at least of which blanks, or more probably both, you will be able to fill up from an inn near your own residence), you must have observed, and doubtless with sympathetic pain, the reluctant agony with which the poor jades at first apply their galled necks to the collars of the harness. But when the irrestible arguments of the post-boy have prevailed on them to proceed a mile or two, they will become callous to the first sensation; and being *warm in the harness*, as the said post-boy may term it, proceed as if their withers were altogether unwrung. This simile so much corresponds with the state of Waverley's feelings in the course of this memorable evening, that I prefer it (especially as being, I trust, wholly original) to any more splendid illustration with which Byshe's Art of Poetry might supply me.[16]

The embarrassment Scott shows here occurs again, where he encounters the problem of describing the process by which Waverley transfers his affections from Flora to Rose. Instead of presenting the process itself – which would have required him to realise states of consciousness over a period of time – Scott fixes on one event when Flora intimates to Waverley that his pursuit of her is hopeless, in the context of a debate on the inconstancy of Romeo. On his way home, Edward is reported as deciding to abandon one love, if not to assume another – ' "I will love my Rosalind no more," said he: "she has given me a broad enough hint for that; and I will speak to her brother and resign my suit. But for a Juliet . . . why then *alors comme alors*." '[17] This typical device of reported soliloquy inevitably has the result of making Waverley seem foolish and insensitive – for which Scott finds an excuse at the beginning of the next chapter. It is a defect which undermines the effectiveness of the whole novel.

This structural weakness is all the more difficult to explain because Scott himself was very much aware of it. It is quite clear that he was prepared to accept a purely mechanical type of construction, in spite of his very substantial commitment to the seriousness and importance of what he was saying – which in the case of *Waverley* at least was beyond doubt.[18] In fact, however, there is a deeper inconsistency in the novel, which helps to suggest an answer to the problem. The presentation of Edward's story depends on a sharp antithesis between imagination and judgement, romantic self-indulgence and realistic self-discipline. According to this view of life, the individual finds happiness only by restraining passion and imagination. Yet the effect of the novel as a whole is very different. The problem for Fergus MacIvor and his sister, or for Baron Bradwardine, is certainly not capable of being presented in the crude terms employed in the description of Waverley. It is certainly not true to suggest that the rebels are romantic or self-indulgent. Nor are they necessarily passionate in their loyalty or self-interest. When we look closely at the novel, in fact, we cannot help feeling that it embodies two separate attitudes to character. In presenting Waverley, Scott was approaching the problems which arose from a contemplation of the rebellion rather than from the rebellion itself. Edward Waverley comes to terms with himself and with the world in which he lives – a world which does not offer opportunities for heroic action or sublime devotion. In his presentation of the characters who are involved in the rebellion otherwise than by chance, Scott emphasises mixture of motives. Above all, he shows us how they are each conditioned by their environment, relationships and upbringing Yet, at the same time, he gives us the impression that their world does offer opportunities for the complete integration of consciousness and action, of sublime devotion, like that of Evan Maccombich, and for heroic resignation, like that of Baron Bradwardine.

This view of character is essentially Romantic, resulting from an imaginative perception of the individual as an end in himself. For its fullest expression it required a fiction that was organic rather than mechanical. Similarly with the central experience of the hero – his self-discovery required to be displayed as if from within, rather than through intermittent reportage. But Scott failed to appreciate even the most basic point in Romantic attitudes to art – he could not accept the essential seriousness of fiction. This failure resulted from his fundamental suspicion of self-consciousness and the imagination. He felt that these qualities were antagonistic to other factors in human character on which happiness depended. His comment on Byron, with whom he deeply sympathised and to some extent identified himself, rests on the assumption that the imagination is a dangerous force:

A powerful and unbridled imagination is the author and architect of its own disappointments. Its fascinations, its exaggerated pictures of good and evil, and the mental distress to which they give rise, are the natural and necessary evils attending on that quick susceptibility of feeling and fancy incidental to the poetical temperament. But the Giver of all talents, while he has qualified them each with its separate and peculiar alloy, has endowed them with the power of purifying and refining them. As if to moderate the arrogance

or genius, it is justly and wisely made requisite, that the conscious possessor must regulate and tame the fire of his fancy,
and descend from the heights to which she exalts him in
order to obtain ease of mind and tranquility. The materials
of happiness, that is, or such degree of happiness as is consistent with our present state, lie around us in profusion. But
they lie so low, that the man of talents must stoop to gather
them; and it is beyond the reach of the mass of society, for
whose benefit, as well as for his, Providence has created them.
There is no royal, and no poetical path to contentment and
heart's ease; that by which they are obtained is open to all
classes of mankind, and lies within the most limited range of
intellect. To narrow our wishes and desires within the scope
of our powers and of attainment . . . to stoop, in short, to the
realities of life; repent if we have offended and pardon if we
have been trespassed against . . . such seem the most obvious
and certain means of keeping or regaining mental tranquility.[19]

This passage tells us a good deal about the author of *Waverley*.
His attitudes are closely similar in some ways to those of later
Realists, who returned to his work for constant inspiration and
encouragement. But later writers learnt from the Romantic
poets that the imagination was the only means of apprehending
reality and came to think that individual happiness and understanding were to be achieved through the fullest development
of the human faculties rather than their subordination to the
convenience of society and the advantages of civilisation as a
whole. Consequently they were obliged to abandon the
mechanical conception of structure which he preserved. Had
Scott himself done this he would have secured his reputation
beyond the nineteenth century and justified the enthusiasm of
contemporaries who compared him to Shakespeare.

Yet it needs to be remembered that the peculiar deficiencies
of his work are the necessary condition on which we possess it
at all. The most fundamental characteristic of his fiction, and

the basis of its originality and strength, was its combination of abstraction and particularity. In one sense, as Duncan Forbes has put it, the Waverley novels can be called 'the triumph of Romanticism', and in another, 'a triumph of the historical thought of the rationalist eighteenth century':

> In Scott this thought blossoms, fertilized and bodied forth in concrete form by the imaginative grasp and creative energy of a great novelist. The result is that unique blend of sociology and romance, of 'philosophical' history and the novelist's living world of individuals, of the general and the particular, in which lies the peculiar genius of Sir Walter Scott.[20]

It was the reductive and anti-romantic aspects of his thinking, reinforcing the native sharpness of vision and memory stored with legend, folk-tale and personal anecdote, that allowed him to make this completely original synthesis. In his case, as in Austen's, the common-sense and critical attitudes of the late eighteenth century, working explicitly in favour of reaction, actually produced a vision of life so original and profound that it worked like a yeast for a half a century or more in England, Germany, France and Spain.

Part II

4 Romantic to Victorian: the Novel after Scott

The Victorian novelist was the direct heir of the English Romantic poets, but his inheritance was not easily won. Potentially it was a problem rather than a solution to problems, and before it could be properly exploited a difficult process of assimilation and adaptation had to take place. This is the reason for the intervention between two periods of intense and sustained achievement in literature of a phase of relative slackness, during which sustained achievement seems to have been extremely difficult. As far as the novel is concerned, this might be seen as the continuing effects of the commitment to the moralistic conceptions of the late eighteenth century. But as A. W. Benn has pointed out, we have to explain a problem which affected not only novelists, but all artists and intellectuals of the period from 1820 to 1845.[1] We might explain it partly in terms of biography – the premature death of Keats (1821), Shelley (1822), and Byron (1824) – but we have little evidence to suggest that any of these three were close to solving their own difficulties about the organisation of longer narrative works. In fact the problem lies deeper. The artist of the period 1820-45 was closely dependent on his predecessors, to whom he looked for education and consolation. But he was also aware that he was facing new conditions and new problems, to which their work offered no immediate solution. The late 1820s and 1830s in England witnessed a sustained effort to assimilate Romantic values to contemporary experience in the realms of theology, social theory, ethics and philosophy. At this time those who thought most deeply about literature and life struggled to work out a critical view of experience according to the positive, Romantic, idea of criticism. During this process the characteristic features of Victorian sensibility and Victorian literary culture emerged and it was on the foundations laid at this time that the achievement of later novelists rested. While it lasted, however, though the novel was often felt to be particularly appropriate to contemporary experience, neither novel nor poem offered adequate scope for those who worked at the deepest level – and those whose experience was more superficial inevitably failed to realise the difficulty that had to be surmounted before it could be made to work properly for them.

Contemporary writers who wanted to adapt the novel to the needs of modern society got little help from their predecessors. Jane Austen, though often praised for her accurate portrayal of manners and characters, seemed in the years after her death to offer no guidance to novelists interested in wider views of life and more overtly profound ideas. Scott's contribution was more fairly appreciated. Contemporaries felt that the effect of his fiction had been to further an organic view of character and society. On the other hand, reference was often made to his dual failure to cope with the problems of contemporary life or to represent the texture of *internal* experience. The lack of guidance in these respects was all the more serious because the overall effect of his career had been to increase the status and the popularity of the novel to the point when it was felt to be capable of more than he had made it perform. Expectations were high among novel readers and critics in the 1820s and 1830s; some even thought that the novel's heyday had already come. So Letitia Landon, a novelist with a substantial contemporary reputation as a poetess, made one of her heroes announce the novel's dominance over other literary forms as early as 1831:

Who, that reflects at all, can deny, that the novel is the literary Aaron's rod that is rapidly swallowing all the rest. It has supplied the place of the drama – it has merged in its pages pamphlets, essays, and satires. Have we a theory, it is developed by means of a character; an opinion – it is set forth in dialogue; and satire is personified in a chapter, not a scene. Poetry has survived somewhat longer, but is rapidly following the fate of its fellows. Descriptions, similes, pathos are to be found in the prose pages and rhythm is becoming more and more an incumbrance rather than a recommendation. I do believe in a little time, lyrical will be the only form of poetry retained . . .[2]

All this passage really shows, however, apart from L. E. L.'s high expectations, is the undeniable fact that the contemporary novel was extending its range and adopting new methods. Throughout her short literary career and beyond, there was continuous experiment and a good deal of vitality in the novel. What was almost totally lacking was the attempt fully to integrate subject-matter with structure. Many novelists tried to deal with serious contemporary problems, aspects of experience never treated before in prose fiction, but almost no one tried to apply the deepest lesson that Scott had taught – that the novelist's material must have the validity and authenticity of history – least of all did they face the forbidding task of assimilating this with the organic conception of art put forward by the Romantic poets. This was the work of a whole generation.

For at least a decade after Jane Austen's death, there was no sign that the nature of this task was even vaguely understood. For most novelists the attractions of the novel were still what they had always been: 'busy crowded and intricate plot; well contrived and fortunate rencontres, which by violent excitement and striking contrasts keep up the reader's strong interests in alternation of painful suspense and delighted discovery'.[3] Even the most serious and progressive writers accepted the mechanistic assumptions of eighteenth century critics. William

Godwin is an example. His *Caleb Williams* (1794) was deeply
convincing on one level because it dramatised the working of
subconscious psychological pressures but was seriously weakened
by its failure in superficial matters of probability. His later
works[4] were far more self-conscious and sophisticated and
through them he carried a good deal further his analysis of
motivation and characters, but they failed far more seriously
than *Caleb Williams* because they embodied a mechanistic idea
of plot and structure, degenerating into inflated dialogue,
impossible behaviour and tormented intrigue.

In a rather humbler sphere the Tory Scot, John Galt, is
another interesting example. In some of his works Galt produced
a kind of fiction which had substantial originality and power.
The attempt to do for Scotland what the *Vicar of Wakefield*
had done for England led him to develop a sustained autobiographical portrait, which produces a strong sense of the
identity of the speaker, indirectly comments on the nature of
identity itself, on the relation between character and environment and between innate character patterns and the course of
the individual's life. Galt was aware that he had produced
something original, but was unable to develop it. He categorised
his *Annals of the Parish* and *The Provost* as a 'a kind of local
theoretical history', which could not really be classed as novels
because of their deficiencies 'as stories':[5]

> They would be more properly characterised, in several in-
> stances, as theoretical histories, than either as novels or
> romances. A consistent fable is essential to a novel as a plot
> is to a drama, and yet those, which were deemed my best
> productions, are deficient in this essential ingredient. . . .
> For example, in the *Annals of the Parish*, there is nothing
> that properly deserves to be regarded as a story; for the only
> link of cohesion, which joins the incidents together, is the
> mere remembrance of the supposed author, and nothing
> makes the work complete within itself, but the biographical
> recurrence upon the scene, of the same individuals. It is, in

consequence, as widely different from a novel, as a novel can be from any other species of narrative.[6]

Significantly, Galt shared Scott's dislike of fantasy, liked Schiller's *The Robbers* and Goethe's *Werther*, but not his later works, and greatly admired Mrs Radcliffe's *Italian*.[7] His idea of the imagination was completely mechanistic – 'Man can only combine the old together'[8] – and the works he described as novels, composed on this principle, are frigid, contorted and grotesque, lacking all the life and vitality his 'theoretical histories' still retain.

Godwin and Galt, though they wrote through the second and third decades of the new century, were essentially men of the old. But younger writers showed no more sensitivity to the most fundamentally revolutionary ideas that had been put forward in the work of Wordsworth and Coleridge and had been commonplace throughout the German speaking world for more than a generation. Frederick Marryatt, for example, ended his career as nothing more than a writer of adventure novels and children's books because of this failure. Marryatt, no doubt, would never have been a profound artist, but he could have been a more serious one, and his undeniable fluency and narrative gifts would in that case have been put to more substantial use. In the early years of his career Marryatt, though in a disorganised way, showed himself aware of some of the most problematic areas of contemporary experience. His young heroes come up against a very raw kind of experience. They suffer not only the inability to adapt to their environment but the difficulty of coping with themselves. In these early novels the hero can find himself painfully torn between crudely conceived moral and sentimental values and personal hardships based on sexual need. Unfortunately as he gained experience Marryatt dropped these elements from his fiction. His idea of the novel either prevented him from facing the difficulties they involved or served as an excuse for a failure based on artistic weakness. He fell back on a mechanistic idea of the novel derived princi-

pally from Le Sage but without any idea of the particular preoccupations of the French novelist for which his techniques
had been subtly appropriate. In Marryatt's conception no novel
could be better than, or ought to be different from, *Gil Blas*:

> It is a faithful copy from real life, and in perfect harmony.
> It is the only novel of which we can assert so much. Others
> may have in some points more merit, but at the same time,
> they have more imperfections. On the whole we must decide
> that *Gil Blas* is the best novel extant.[9]

By contrast to *Gil Blas* even *Don Quixote* took second place –
Cervantes made a greater display of art; 'but in *Gil Blas* we have
a truer copy of *nature*'.[10]

Marryatt's ideas about the novel, for all the harm they may
have done him as a novelist, at any rate included a high degree
of respect for his predecessors. A picture of the novel in the
first half of the nineteenth century in England would be incomplete if it did not show the degree to which, even as late as
1841, it was possible to write seriously and be taken
seriously from a standpoint that was fifty years out of date.
Robert Plumer Ward is of interest now only because his first
novel, *Tremaine* (1825), like Godwin's *Fleetwood* (1805), an
attempt to adapt the form of Mackenzie's *Man of Feeling* to
permit an analysis of modern subjectivism, influenced Edward
Bulwer Lytton and Benjamin Disraeli, encouraging them to
begin as novelists. In his day, however, Ward was an important
figure, whose attempt to raise the status of the novel and to
show the relationship between personality, morality and political and social circumstances was taken seriously by all the leading magazines. And in his *De Clifford* in 1841, Ward still
thought it appropriate to make an evidently sensible character
launch into a condemnation of all the best novels of the past
on grounds of their moral effect.

> The worst is, these seducers, both English and French (Field-
> ing, Smollett, Rousseau), approach us so entirely in the garb of

friends, are so set off with wit, humour, agreeableness, and
the semblance of virtue, though deeply mingled with vice, that
we are taken before we are aware and incur the woe de-
nounced by the prophet on those who call evil good and good
evil.
Like the transformed monsters in *Comus*,
> 'So perfect is our misery,
> We boast ourselves more lovely than before'.[11]

Practising novelists who wrote partly for their living, like
Marryatt and Ward, Lady Morgan, Frances Trollope, Mrs Gore,
could not have been expected to have thought very profoundly
about either their art or about life in general. What profundity
and coherence such writers possess must obviously descend from
above, and as far as writers of their stamp are concerned, there
must have been a considerable lapse of time before Romantic
ideas about the nature of life and its relationship with art were
sufficiently well established to affect their work. In the 1830s,
however, there was no one for them to learn from. Writers of
greater ability and deeper understanding were no more capable
of continuing the achievement of the Romantic poets than their
inferiors. At first sight this is the more surprising because they
were preoccupied to the point of obsession with Romantic
literature. We remember Tennyson weeping over Byron's grave
and Browning caught up in uncritical adoration of the spirit
revealed in the pages of the pirated edition of Shelley's work.
Disraeli's preoccupation with Byron and Shelley led him to
write a fictionalised version of their lives, explaining and
palliating the internal strains and tensions that had led to their
alienation from the English public. Edward Bulwer Lytton's
comment on his own reaction to Byron's death shows the degree
of his involvement with the whole body of Romantic poetry:

Never shall I forget the singular, the stunning sensation,
which the intelligence produced. I was exactly at that age,
half man and half boy, in which the poetical sympathies are
most keen – among the youth of that day a growing diver-

C

sion from Byron to Shelley and Wordsworth had just commenced – but the moment in which we heard he was no
more, united him to us at once, without a rival. We could
not believe that the bright race was run. So much of us died
with him that the notion of his death had something of the
unnatural, of the impossible. It was as if a part of the
mechanism of the very world stood still.[12]

Not all Lytton's contemporaries were as emotional as he was in
his adolescence. Nor did they all owe a great deal to the
Romantic poets. Thomas Carlyle, a notorious exception, formed
his mind under the influence of German literature and metaphysics, and many others looked to the same source, followed
Friedrich Schlegel to Cervantes and Shakespeare, or studied the
English divines and poets of the seventeenth century. The reputation of Bacon rose again at this time, as he came to be looked
on as a writer who combined rationalist methods with an
awareness of life as an organic whole. The poetry of Wordsworth, Shelley and Coleridge was but the most common source
of the same inspiration.

   Not all Romantic poets were positively helpful. Increasingly
after the 1820s, Byron's influence was felt to be harmful. His
poetry reflected, as in a dark mirror, the worst aspects of the
artist's personality rather than the best. It reflected what was
felt to be a morbid connection between youthful idealism and
hopefulness, indulgent self-worship and cynical criticism. On
the other hand, Wordsworth's poetry was a continuing resource
to artists and thinkers. It offered implicit assurance of the unity
and meaningfulness of experience and the brotherhood of man.
Shelley kept alive the highest political ideals derived from
Romantic doctrine and showed their connection with the purest
feelings and impulses of heart and mind. But it was probably
through the prose work of Coleridge that Romantic ideas were
most widely and explicitly disseminated. John Sterling credited
Coleridge with introducing him to the most important ideas of
the time: 'To Coleridge I owe *education*. He taught me to

believe that an empirical philosophy is none, that Faith is the Highest Reason, that all criticism, whether of literature, laws or manners, is blind, without the power of discerning the organic unity of the object.'[13] A modern commentator explains the importance of Coleridge's function at this time as a conductor of the central tenets of Romanticism through coherent and rational argument:

> It was his restoration of human feelings to their rightful place, and his triumphant vindication of personality, that gave Coleridge his peculiar power . . . These two notes were sounded with telling effect, after Coleridge had found a philosophical basis for his faith, in the work of Kant and his successors. He found that every impression is accompanied by a corresponding feeling, a state of the whole being, which is an integral part of experience. Man is not a mere sum of his impressions, thoughts and emotions, but a something greater than all these. The basis of this entity is the will, and the colour of it is the characteristic set of feelings incident to its experience. For feeling is the visible essence of personality. In promulgating these doctrines *qua* philosopher, Coleridge exerted an indirect but powerful influence.[14]

Essentially the same view could be got from other sources – even from the novels of Scott. Coleridge was especially helpful because he treated Romantic ideas explicitly and because he had tried himself to extend them outside literature.

The continuation of this task was the business of the next generation of writers, but in the altered circumstances in which they lived, it was not the basis of confidence and security so much as a new and painful problem in itself. The Romantic movement, in so far as there had been one at all, had failed to affect the surface of English life, or its institutions. During the Napoleonic wars the Establishment remained conservative – conservative Tory, or conservative Whig, along the lines indicated by the *Quarterly* and *Edinburgh* reviews, representing the unreasoning alliance to outworn institutions or the

criticism of those institutions according to rationalist principles
in alliance with Whig interests. After the war a new spirit was
at work in the country, which worked at its deepest level in
the same direction as the ideas of Romantic artists, but seemed
on the surface to be creating sharper divisions and conflicts. As
Edward Bulwer Lytton describes it, this new spirit was the
desire for utility:

> Insensibly acted upon by the doctrine of the Utilitarians,
> we desired to see Utility in every branch of intellectual
> labour. Byron, in his severe comments upon England, and
> his satire on our social system, had done much that has not
> yet been observed, in shaking off from the popular mind
> certain of its strongest national prejudices; and the long
> Peace, and the pressure of financial difficulties, naturally in-
> clined us to look narrowly at our real estate: to examine
> the laws we had only boasted of, and dissect the constitution
> we had hitherto deemed it only our duty to admire. We were
> in the situation of a man who, having run a certain career of
> dreams and extravagance, begins to be prudent and saving, to
> calculate his conduct, and to look at his estate. Politics thus
> gradually and commonly absorbed our attention, and we
> grew to identify ourselves, our feelings and our cause, with
> statesmen and economists instead of with poets and refiners.
> Thus, first Canning, and then Brougham, may be said, for a
> certain time, to have represented, more than any other
> individuals, the common Intellectual spirit; and the interest
> usually devoted to the imaginative, was transferred to the
> real.[15]

In reaction from the period of isolation and traditionalism that
preceded 1815, reform movements gathered momentum. People
began to talk about, and even to effect, the rationalisation of
the political and social systems so as to give representation to the
new industrial towns and the new classes associated with
industry and commerce. At the same time, reform was required
and produced in criminal law, government of the Colonies,

economics and taxation. Finally, behind the conservative reform of the late 1820s came the movement for Political reform which united the middle and lower sections of the population. Utilitarians and Philosophic Radicals represented this new phase of rationalist reform and gained for a short time an influence quite out of proportion with their numerical strength.[16] As Bulwer Lytton explained, in *England and the English*, this upsurge of rationalism was only one other symptom of the general shift in values which had produced Romanticism itself. In mid-century Realism the Romantics' organic view of society and human character drew on the methods of scientific research and the principles of rationalist enquiry for its support. But in the 1820s and 1830s the widespread emphasis on practical reform helped to increase the isolation of those who inherited the Romantic mistrust of rationalism.

In the meantime, the religious revival introduced new sources of strain which further complicated the artist's situation. By the 1820s Evangelicalism had spread out from small pressure groups to affect the whole Church, bringing from eighteenth century Methodism a new seriousness and a greater stress on the individual's spiritual awareness. As the Church took on the enormous missionary task of serving the new industrial population it brought theology into direct conflict with social and economic factors from which it had previously been isolated. At the same time, even while it was eventually learning to cope with the eighteenth century attacks on religion, it came into contact with new forms of rationalist enquiry which often provoked crises of faith. More serious still, because it stressed the individual's sense of sin, encouraged self-examination and tended to postpone until manhood the adolescent's sharp encounter with the realities of human character and economic life, Evangelicalism contributed greatly to the particularly English form of the *mal de siècle* which affected artists and thinkers increasingly at this time.[17]

This general malaise had its root in the persistent dilemma facing the Romantic temperament. Truth, it seemed, could only be apprehended by the individual sensitive to nature, to human passion, and who possessed a high degree of self-consciousness. Self-preoccupation, however, seemed to lead inexorably to self-doubt, a loss of contact with the springs of life outside the individual and consequent depression and sterility. In the early nineteenth century, after self-awareness had been heightened by the experience of Romantic poetry, especially that of Byron, and intensified for many by being given a religious dimension, the degree of confusion and distress seemed to contemporaries to exceed by far anything felt by the archetypal Werther or the mournful hero of Chateaubriand's tales. Outside the context of religious debate we have the famous case of John Stuart Mill, whose depression brought him to the verge of suicide before he was saved by an access of emotion, which came first through a reading of Marmontel, and was deepened and sustained by the poetry of Wordsworth. After crisis came his friendship with Mrs Taylor and the revitalisation of his emotional life which had direct and immediate effects on the direction of his intellectual development, leading him increasingly to modify his Utilitarian doctrine to allow for the importance of the organic life of the individual and the nation and finally, under Mrs Taylor's direct influence, towards socialism. A more dramatic instance of the same crisis, accentuated by religious worries, occurred to the unlikely personage of Richard Chenevix Trench, future Archbishop of Dublin and a pillar of the Irish Church during her most difficult years. Trench was a friend of F. D. Maurice and John Sterling, and he had written satirically about the latter's self-doubts and questionings. Later he regretted his condemnation of Sterling, when the same condition overcame him.

> . . . it is with this as with all my feelings, that I have led myself to contemplate them as separable parts of myself, not to be content with loving till I knew why I loved, not to enjoy pleasure till I could discover why it pleased. And, as a due punishment, love remains to me only in the forms which my

understanding first leads to, and pleasure only in the meagre skeleton of a metaphysical definition. I would give up my hopes of an eternity almost, if I could fall passionately, ay, madly in love at this moment. It might make my prayers pass out of the narrow sphere which binds them to earth, and lies like a thick robe between me and God. In reading over what I have written, I am ready to laugh with scorn and contempt and hatred at myself; I forsooth, who abused Sterling for his self-abusing letters and in the pride of my unfeelingness talked about calm minds and well-balanced spirits.

I have been reading Wordsworth, and am all the better for it. Poetry is religion, and so, if there be any truth in philosophy, must all the living powers of the soul be . . .[18]

Trench's *cri de coeur* is unusual in its intensity, but only in that. His dilemma was that of many of the best of his contemporaries. Life in general seemed increasingly problematic to them; but their own particular existence presented an immediate problem which had to be solved as a matter of urgency. The prototype of the early nineteenth century intellectual suffering from the impossibility of living simply and naturally, of feeling or believing instinctively and without doubt, was the Ancient Mariner. But his case was easier to understand in that it was brought about by a symbolic crime. Coleridge's *Dejection, an Ode* was clearly a central text in the literature which described the condition. From both Wordsworth and Coleridge, in fact, the early nineteenth century thinker could derive consolation and sustaining hope. But their experience was too highly subjective to provide the basis of a solution to the problem in society at large. Some further course had to be discovered which could permit the individual to remain a thinking being and to escape alienation from his own feelings and from the world around him. The answer came through modifying the romantic conception of love. Following, perhaps, the hints of Wordsworth himself in the lines extolling the gentle influence of Dorothy in the *Prelude*,[19] his successors made the emotion which for him had been identifiable with the Imagination, itself the means of revitalising emotional life, integrating the individual, and re-unifying him with the society in which he lived. In doing this, as a necessary step, they also created the Victorian woman, unintellectual, undemanding, pure and confident in the power of faith and charity. The process is seen at work in a late story by John Sterling, where the prototype of an endless series of Agnes Whitfields and Laura Bells soothes the hero's tortured mind in calm and unreflecting embraces. Sterling's hero has lost his faith, but in Elizabeth's presence he recovers it, and throws off the 'damned vacillating state' which affected so many sensitive contemporaries:

> I have now seen Elizabeth many times. Her whole life and culture have had but the two elements, the domestic and the Biblical. Yet to how complete, and melodius, nay, sometimes how high and lyrical a being has she attained! She knows little indeed; but she has the most open, the freshest, and the truest sense for whatever is natural and worthy, While with her, and thinking no longer of speculations, or of myself, I feel as if I had thrown off a stiff and heavy armour, which I had worn for years, and been clad of a sudden in soft and lucid silken robes. On how divine is the blessedness of love! It leaves me no fear and regrets. I feel that life is indeed a capacity for joy, and is nothing else.[20]

With his Elizabeth the early Victorian intellectual, like the hero of late Victorian novels, could find a measure of peace and fulfilment. He could feel at one and the same time that he was restored through his mistress to contact with the world which lay beyond the reach of analytic reason, and that he was, through the ceremony of marriage, integrated with the community in which he lived, itself the largest visible emblem of the unity which transcends sense:

> This is a great blessing of marriage, that it delivers us from the tyranny of *Meum* and *Teum*. Converting each into the

other, it endears them both, and turns a slavish deadening drudgery into a free and joyous service. And by bringing home to every one's heart, that he is something better than a mere self, that he is the part of a higher and more precious whole, it becomes a type of the union between the Church and her Lord.

———— ————

To Adam Paradise was home. To the good among his descendants, home is Paradise.[21]

The evolution of the Victorian wife and the Victorian sister – as Julius Hare revealingly called her, 'the best of earthly moral antiseptics' – were indications of a prevailing tendency to identify and resolve sources of tension in contemporary experience. John Stuart Mill, in his essays on Bentham and Coleridge, shows the same tendency. Mill identifies his subjects as types of widespread forces at work in contemporary culture – the spirit of rationalism which works for progress and the conservative tendency which remains content with the nature of things as they exist. Though he was brought up entirely within the rationalist tradition, Mill's view of this changed. After the crisis in his personal life and partly as a result of his friendships with Maurice and Carlyle, he came to think that it was the primary objective of the intellectual in his day to unify the principles represented by Bentham and Coleridge. In wider terms the desire to unify the principle of rational analysis and scientific methods of establishing the truth about man's nature and his environment, with the belief in the necessity of apprehending human life as a whole, the spiritual with the physical, came to be one of the central characteristics of Victorian literature. Mill is untypical only in the relatively narrow range of his reflections, and in the fact that he arrived at the conclusion that a unified view was necessary only after a long process of development.

It was more common in the literature of the period to see the idea that life was essentially unified taken as the starting point in a process which stretched over a much wider front and led

C*

to the consolidation of a view in which all aspects of contemporary experience were pieced together. Julius Hare is more typical of the early Victorian thinker in this respect than Mill. After an early volume of aphorisms Hare produced little literary work except translations from German and occasional sermons and polemical articles, but he made the sermons he preached at Cambridge the vehicle of a subtle and persuasive theological view, which rested on a thorough mastery of the culture of his own country and an understanding of the evolution of modern European society as a whole. What Hare did, in effect, was to apply Romantic principles to the analysis of the modern situation and then to equate the terminology derived from Romantic literature and German criticism with the concepts of Anglican theology. So he was able to build up a view of human existence as an organic whole, at the centre of which, and throughout which, Cambridge undergraduates could be encouraged to find, not the Romantic Imagination but the Word of God.

In the first place Hare agreed with Goethe and Carlyle that the predominant characteristic of the modern period was its subjectivity:

This pervades all the forms of life, all the regions of thought. There has been a far deeper selfconsciousness, which has often approacht to a selfdevouring disease: there has been a more minute self-analysis, a more piercing self-anatomy. Speculation has turned its eyes inward, has become more and more reflective. If we cast a look on the two main provinces of intellect in the great age which followed the Reformation, we find that in Philosophy the grand achievement of that age was the purifying the method of investigation, the gaining a deeper insight into the laws of thought. Whereafter in another generation Consciousness was asserted to be the ground of all existence; and an attempt was made to expand the proposition, that Thought involves Being, into a complete system of philosophy. Hence by various steps men mounted to the denial of all reality; until at the apex of the pyramid

Self took its stand, as its own self-existent world, its own creative god. Meanwhile, as the natural counterpart of this exhausted idealism, the materialist equally denied all moral realities, and made out that the apparations of all such things are nothing else than a fantasmagoria played off by the magic lantern of self-interest.[22]

Self-consciousness, commonly extended to self-preoccupation, impeded virtue and threatened the workings of the imagination. While the individual was committed to self, Hare argued, his life could never be meaningful. The distortion involved in self-preoccupation prevented him from satisfying the deepest need, of his nature – the desire for unity:

> The desire of unity is inherent in man. It pervades all the expressions, all the modifications of his being, and may in a manner be termed an elementary principle of his nature. It lies, very often without his being conscious of it, at the bottom of all the workings of his mind, which is ever seeking, in one way or other, to infuse unity into the objects of its contemplation . . .[23]

The painfulness of experience arose, Hare thought, from the fact that it seems to defy this deepest need, corresponding to what Coleridge called the Primary Imagination:

> That this desire of beholding unity in all things arises from that unity of consciousness, in which man was made, and in which his Maker mirrored His own unity, cannot well be doubted. But while we have this principle of unity within us, we are set in the midst of a world, in which everything, when we first look out over it, seems to jar and war against all unity, a world which at first sight may seem to be just emerging or subsiding out of Chaos.[24]

This primary consciousness, which should replace the usurping self-consciousness, could only be attained and could only be fully expressed through faith, which combined the world of action and the world of spirit, through will. Faith, Hare said, continuing with strongly Coleridgean terminology, 'proceeds from the inmost depths of the soul, from beyond that firmament of Consciousness, whereby the waters under the firmament are divided from the waters above the firmament. It is the act of that living principle, which constitutes each man's individual, continuous, immortal personality',[25] Religious faith, expressed in membership of the Anglican Church, thus constitutes identity, consciousness, or being itself. It is the means by which Victorian man can escape the problems of his age and achieve communion with the living God, worshipped through the established Church, instead of the mysterious powers of nature, encountered in Romantic bower or moorland.

The arguments found in Hare's sermons are minor examples of the tendencies working throughout contemporary literature in the period which followed the publication of the first series of Waverley novels and the death of Jane Austen. Frederick Denison Maurice and Thomas Carlyle are more significant examples because the breadth and depth of their work is greater, their influence wider spread and their literary achievement longer lasting. Essentially, however, all three represent the same tendency. In their work we can see clearly what was happening less clearly elsewhere – the transformation of Romantic values so as to make them the basis of a coherent view of life, including physical and metaphysical, psychological, moral and social elements. The basic pattern which resulted from this process emerged early on, and significantly the novel was used as its vehicle. But at this stage, though we could say that in the novels of Edward Bulwer Lytton the Realist ethos had already taken shape, one element essential to the development of Realism was missing. In the Victorian novel the action has the authority of a natural history of contemporary life. The Realist ethos, insisting that all life is integrated and coherent, laying down the terms for which the individual's life may be so, and attacking departures from the moral principles on which social life should be governed, was then eventually seen to be justified in the only way possible. The principle of unity expressed itself through the structure and the texture of the experience concerned. This achievement, though partial in many cases, resulted from a confident understanding of the nature of life, its values and principles, which was the possession not only of the isolated artists of originality and power, but of men and women of lesser note. Such a confidence, so widely diffused, could not have grown quickly. It depended partly on a general appreciation of the quality and significance of Romantic poetry of the preceding period, but it derived more immediately from the experiments and the struggles of the 1820s and the 1830s – from the series of attempts, few of which were successful, to achieve a coherent view of human life in the contemporary world.

5 Edward Bulwer Lytton: Aspiration and Disaster

Edward Bulwer Lytton was typical of the best and worst of his age. He was a very prolific and popular author, widely respected in his own time. Between his seventeenth year and his thirty-seventh, which marks a turning point in his career, Lytton produced six volumes of poems, five plays and thirteen novels, a number of pamphlets and a great deal of journalism and miscellaneous writings of various kinds. His novels cover the whole range of fiction produced in the period, including Byronic confession, novels of fashionable life, historical novels, Newgate novels and *romans à clef*. An active politician on the liberal side throughout the time, he also produced in *England and the English* (1833) a comprehensive and thoughtful survey of contemporary culture and society. In many respects his work was original and admirable. He thoroughly understood the importance of the changes which had been taking place in literature, society and politics, appreciated the leading qualities and fundamental achievement of the English Romantic poets and their German contemporaries and was among the very first writers who faced the task of adapting their values to contemporary English society. In his early fiction he showed himself aware of the forces at work in England, attacked the materialism and increasing snobbery which seemed to be accompanying them, and struck out in his poems and novels a philosophic and moral view which anticipates the leading features of the Victorian outlook. He also appreciated the importance of the novel and was the first novelist to project a theory of fiction based on organic conceptions. Yet while he did all this, he failed, by no small margin, to produce fiction of lasting interest. For all his theorising about the organic integrity of the novel Lytton still remained satisfied with mechanical techniques, arbitrary manipulation, sensational and melodramatic presentation of character.

Lytton identified the leading feature of his age as the spirit of benevolence, which saw as the deeper current underlying the desire for Utility which had emerged as the dominant tendency on the surface. 'Some cause, indeed, there is of fear,' he he argued in *England and the English,* 'lest the desire for immediate and palpable utility should stint the capacities of genius to the trite and familiar truths. But as Criticism takes a more wide and liberal view of the true and unbounded sphere of the Beneficial, we may trust that this cause of fear will be removed'.[1] It was through benevolence, he argued, that true utility was to be achieved and social advancement assured. His political alignment with progressive parties enabled him to appreciate that such advancement was only to be achieved through rationalist reorganisation of society. Yet at the same time, through his appreciation of Romantic poetry he was able to see the movement in its wider implications, avoid the narrowness of the Utilitarians and Philosophic Radicals and suggest a path by which they might be humanised: 'There has grown up amongst us a sympathy with the great mass of mankind,' he remarked, a sympathy instilled by poets, philosophers and novelists alike; 'It is this feeling that we should unite to sustain and develop. It has come to us pure and bright from the ordeal of years – the result of a thousand errors, but born, if we preserve it, as their healer and redemption'.[2]

Lytton traced this increasing sympathy with the great mass of mankind to the influence of the Romantic poets. In his age, he thought, literature had assumed 'the natural office of Reason': 'Imaginative Literature has arrogated the due place of the Philosophical'.[3] The advancement of thought had been carried furthest by the work of Shelley and Wordsworth. Lytton saw Byron and Scott dealing with the more superficial passions of mankind, whereas the two former poets gave poetical embodiment to the principles which governed passions themselves. And of these two the influence of Wordsworth was the most beneficial. Wordsworth shared with Goethe 'the reverential, contemplative, self-tasking disposition to the study of all things appertaining to THE NATURAL'.[4] Though Shelley was 'the spiritualizer of all who forsake the past and the present and with lofty hopes and a bold philanthropy, rush forward into the future', he forgot, in Lytton's opinion, the chain by which are linked 'the highest to the lowest, in one indisoluble connexion, that united even the highest heaven to the bosom of our common earth'.[5] On the other hand, in an age which Lytton thought leaned to the material and produced an appetite for coarse excitement, the tendency of Wordsworth's poetry was 'to elevate the mind to contemplate the inner meaning of human life'.

> Wordsworth's poetry is of all existing in the world the most calculated to refine – to etherialize – to exalt; – to offer the most correspondent counterpoise to the scale that inclines to earth. It is for this that I consider his influence mainly beneficial. His poetry has repaired to us the want of an immaterial philosophy – nay it is philosophy, and it is of the immaterial school. No writer more unvulgarises the mind. His circle is small – but for that very reason his votaries are more attached? They preserve in the working-day world the sabbath of his muse – and doubtless they will perpetuate that tranquilising worship from generation to generation, till the devotion of the few shall grow into the custom of the many.[6]

In his own literary work Lytton tried to work out the implications of Wordsworth's poetry. It was one of his first tasks to attack the Byronic indulgence of passions and emotions which led to alienation and cynicism. His admiration for Byron did not prevent him from seeing the sterility of self-preoccupation and implementing Wordsworth's principles by insisting that self-fulfilment could only be attained through relatedness with others, in love, or through devotion to their interests in political service. One of his earliest poems, which centres on an incident from his own experience, takes as its hero a love-lorn youth who reacts from disappointment towards a Shelleyan idea of liberty for the human race. The epigraph to this poem, 'Tale of a Dreamer', shows Lytton's consciousness of the *mal de siècle* which afflicted so many heroes from Werther to Flaubert's Frédéric Moreau: 'Le coeur se blase, les ressorts se brisent, et l'on finit, je crois, par n'être plus sensible à rien'. Lytton's hero loves Viola, who is forced to marry another, pines, declines and dies, and on her deathbed writes to ask him to visit her grave. There he finds strength to escape from the tormented pre-occupation with his own frustrated passion and shakes off the temptation to retire to solitude and curse the conditions of human existence and the rest of the human race:

> But tho' the spirits of that world, are not
> Wild-free – and dark perchance, as is my own; –
> And fain my heart would wish for wings to fly
> Far from my Kind, where Quiet points a spot
> Where first the lone rock and silent sky
> Woo'd the young rapture of my musing eye –
> Yet not for me such solitary joy,
> Grief hath not sear'd my soul to selfishness,
> The Wise alone can shine, the Great destroy –
> But e'en the meanest have the power to bless!

Therefore, he concludes, he still worships freedom:

> Tho' cold my heart for others it shall burn,
> Ardent as when with selfish fires it glow'd.[7]

The principles embodied in this rather feeble plant from *Weeds and Wildflowers* found fuller expression in Lytton's novels. The first of these – *Falkland* (1827), later withdrawn from publication on the grounds that it might encourage in youthful readers the evil it was designed to cure – studied the decline and death of a hero whose early youth brought him to a state of mind not far removed from that which threatened the youthful Waverley. His father dead, he spent his vacations from school in 'a wild and romantic' area where he 'wandered by day over the rude scenes which surrounded us; and at evening I pored, with an unwearied delight, over the ancient legends, which made those scenes sacred to my imagination',[8] Gradually he imbibed the romance of his studies, and in the alternation between the restless activity of school and 'the idleness of reflection', derived an instability of character which vitiated his life.

> Hence not only all intermediums of emotion appear to me as tame, but even the most overwrought excitation can bring neither novelty nor zest. I have, as it were, feasted upon the passions; I have made that my daily food, which in its strength and excess, would have been poison to others; I have rendered my mind unable to enjoy the ordinary aliments of nature; and I have wasted, by a premature indulgence, my resources and my powers, till I have left my heart, without a remedy or a hope, to whatever disorders its own intemperence has ingendered.[9]

In *Falkland* the diseases resulting from excess of self-awareness were presented heroically, though with explicit disapproval. Lytton later came to think of the story as a necessary means of purging himself of the Byronic infection. The next time he used a similar theme he set it in a context of the adventures of a hero who reacts more positively to the problems life brings. The story of Reginald Glanville, melodramatically doomed to premature disintegration from the beginning of the novel, as a result of the same 'acute and sensitive morbidity of mind, which has been and still is, so epidemic a disease', occurs in *Pelham* (1828), Lytton's first and one of his most popular novels. Pelham himself reacts from a loveless home by assuming a mask of foppery, from beneath which he gradually develops a sense of purpose and direction which later enable him to achieve domestic happiness and social usefulness. This is the aim for all Lytton's positive heroes, who learn that to live for self alone is to lose one's life. As the hero's friend, Radclyffe, tells him in another novel, to be happy one must forget oneself:

> Alas! . . . it is no use advising one to be happy who has no object beyond himself. Either enthusiasm, or utter mechanical coldness, is necessary to reconcile men to the cares and mortifications of life. You must feel nothing, or you must feel for others. Unite yourself to a great object; see its goal distinctly; cling to its course courageously; hope for its triumph sanguinely; and on its majestic progress you sail, as in a ship, agitated indeed by the storms, but unheeding the breeze and the surge that would appal the individual effort. The larger public objects make us glide smoothly and unfelt over our minor griefs. To be happy, my dear Godolphin, you must forget yourself. Your refining and poetical temperament preys upon your content. Learn benevolence – it is the only cure to a morbid nature.[10]

Like Godolphin, the contemporary reader might well have been 'greatly struck' by this advice of Radcliffe. In 1833 it came with some force and originality. In the whole series of novels, of which *Godolphin* is one, it continued to be given as the central statement in a view of life designed to reconcile the central ideas of Romantic literature with contemporary circumstances of which the author was keenly aware and in which he was actively engaged.

Lytton also showed originality in his view of the nature of the novel. He understood the concept of organic form and he realised that post-Romantic art needed to concern itself with the nature of internal experience rather than external action. As he conceived the role of the novel it was to establish the inner meaning of human life by examining passions, character and manners, and embody, through the shape of the fiction itself, the patterns existing within experience. He was highly conscious of the deficiency of Sir Walter Scott in this respect. The currently fashionable comparison between Scott and Shakespeare seemed to him to indicate the low state of criticism in the country. While Shakespeare aimed 'at the development of the secret man', 'half distaining the mechanism of external incidents', Lytton said, Scott attempted no more than to paint the ruffles, dress, features and gestures of man. 'Avoiding the movements of the heart, elaborate in the progress of incidents', Scott never caught the mantle of Shakespeare, but he improved on the dresses of his wardrobe and threw artificial effects on to the scenes of his theatres.[11]

Scott's deficiency arose, Lytton thought, from the failure to conceptualise his subject. The artist greater than Scott 'will suffer the subject he selects to lie long in his mind, to be resolved, meditated, brooded over, until from the chaos breaks the light, and he sees distinctly the highest end for which the materials can be used and the best process by which they can be reduced to harmony and order.'[12] With this idea Lytton was able to break completely free of eighteenth century arguments about the morality of fiction and to see the importance of the structural integrity of the work of art as a direct representation of the nature of things. No literary work, in Lytton's view, could be 'at once true and immoral'. On the other hand, the statement of a novel, in order to attain to truth, had to relate to the inner nature of life rather than mere externals. The novel which came nearest to perfection of form was *Gil Blas*; but as one of his more learned characters explains for him in *Pelham*, *Gil Blas* falls short of the highest level of art because it deals only with the surface of things:

'It must require', said Lady Roseville, 'an extraordinary combination of mental powers to produce a perfect novel.' 'One so extraordinary', answered Vincent, 'that though we have one perfect epic poem, and several which pretend to perfection, we have not one perfect novel in the world. *Gil Blas* approaches more nearly to perfection than any other; but it must be confessed that there is a want of dignity, or moral rectitude, and of what I may term moral beauty, through the whole book. If an author could combine the various excellencies of Scott and Le Sage, with a greater and more metaphysical knowledge than either, we might expect from him the perfection we have not yet discovered since the days of Apuleius.'[18]

On this idea Lytton founded his own career as a novelist. He tried to identify and embody the forces at work in society and in politics, to show the development of individual character, acted on by circumstances and universal law, and at the same time to represent the metaphysical basis of true morality and happiness.

This design was formed in its essentials before Lytton was twenty-one and by the time he was thirty it had acquired the proportions of a clear and consistent doctrine. Though it was a composite view, derived from greater writers and completed under the direct influence of Goethe's writings, it was substantially original in its application to Lytton's own country. Yet, when this is said, little more can follow. As a novelist Lytton's dreary failure oddly counterbalances his intellectual success. The originality and coherence of his theory do not prevent him from descending to melodrama, sensationalism, prolixity and rant. Though he saw the novel as organic and integral, he failed to achieve a technique and form appropriate to his subject. Instead, in his endless string of novels, he juggled abstract conceptions, tricked out in the outworn frippery of Gothic romance and melodrama.

Lytton's failure is not difficult to understand if one looks at the novelist from whom he learned his art. Le Sage begins the list and gave his successor the tendency to think of structure in terms of plot. After Le Sage came William Godwin, whose *Cloudesly* Lytton reviewed and with whom he had an enthusiastic correspondence. The two men coincided in their political beliefs and their admiration was mutual. From Godwin Lytton got the plan of *Eugene Aram*.[14] He also admired Thomas Hope and John Moore who, like Godwin, had tried to find means of embodying through fiction a view of the inner nature of human character. They failed, too, for the same reason. They approached the novel as rationalists, working from analytical conceptions, and they thought of form as needing to fulfil absolute conditions of pleasingness rather than as relative to the nature of the novel's statement. Moore's most successful novel, *Zeluco* (1786), studies the condition of wickedness in its effect on the behaviour and personality of one individual. The result is a series of incidents, culminating in the inevitable decline and death of the villian/hero, which has no coherence at all except that given by the author's abstract scheme. Hope's *Anastasius* (1819) is more ambitious and more successful than any novel of Godwin or Moore, but suffers from the same deep-rooted inadequacy. 'The Adventures of a Modern Greek', tracing the gradual degeneration of character and morality, the erosion of the finer qualities by the gradual pressure of circumstances, and the disappointment of hopes and passions, is a finely wrought and well conceived study, but its final effect is boring and disgusting. Hope failed to unify external incident and character analysis, so that the novel breaks down into a seemingly endless sequence of events, the order and arrangement of which have no meaning for the reader except what is given by the coincidence of biography.

As might be expected from the admirer of Godwin, who thought Shakespeare's superiority lay in his conceptual ability, Lytton conceived his novels in terms of an abstract scheme and then laboured to clothe it with suitable action. And as a great admirer of Byron's drama, he tended to choose actions which produced violent confrontations and were held together by theatrical intrigue. Lytton thought of character in terms of types – individuals whose characteristics make them representative of general principles and aspects of the human condition.

Pelham is a young man who turns outwards; Godolphin a young man who turns inwards. Given this starting point, actions had to be devised to show how they would develop under the influence of external laws and forces. *Eugene Aram* shows Lytton's method. The case of a learned murderer, apprehended and executed some years after his crime, excited Lytton's attention because it gave him a chance to investigate certain general traits and tendencies of human character. As he wrote in the preface of the 1840 edition, the apparent lack of motive and the inconsistency between the action and the life and character of the criminal, 'presents an anomaly in human conduct so rare and surprising, that it would be difficult to find any subject more adapted for that metaphysical speculation and analysis, in order to indulge which, Fiction, whether in the drama, or the higher class of romance, seeks its materials and grounds its lessons in the chronicles of passion and crime.'[15] The result, as contemporary critics were quick to observe, was absurd – the representation of an impossible monster, achieved in the first place by distortion of the facts, and bodied forth only with the help of inflated rhetoric and incredible incident.

Eugene Aram is an extreme case, a novel which Lytton greatly altered before republication and which is far from typical of his novels in general. Yet the vices which are obvious there are distinctive characteristics of his work as a whole. By the end of the 1830s Lytton had completed his own education, had assimilated the work of the Romantic poets, made a close study of his own society and culture, taught himself German and mastered the work of Goethe. In two connected novels, *Ernest Maltravers* and *Alice, or The Mysteries* he brought together all that he had learnt, attempting to reproduce the achievement of Goethe in *Wilhelm Meister* in practical and realistic terms. The preface to the first volume reads like similar claims in the preface to Charlotte Brontë's *The Professor* and reminds the reader of the sort of anti-heroic programme outlined in Chapter 17 of *Adam Bede:*

In the hero of this tale thou wilt find neither a majestic demigod, nor a fascinating demon. He is a man with the weaknesses derived from humanity, with the strength that we inherit from the soul; not often obstinate in error, more often irresolute in virtue; sometimes too aspiring, sometimes too despondent; influenced by the circumstances to which he yet struggles to be superior, and changing in character with the changes of time and fate; but never wantonly rejecting those great principles by which alone we can work out the Science of Life – a desire for the Good, a passion for the Honest, a yearning after the True.'[16]

Only with the tell-tale abstractions at the end of the passage do we remember that we are not reading a description of one of a dozen heroes of later Realist novels. In the novel itself the consequences of the tendency to abstraction become more painfully apparent; *Ernest Maltravers* and *Alice* together trace the development of an individual to full maturity and understanding of his own life and the nature of his environment. As novels they fail, in spite of a good deal of interesting writing, sharp observation of contemporary manners, and accurate analysis of the condition of English politics and French culture. The failure results directly from the fact that their action is entirely externalised, while the actual subject – inner development of the hero through personal relations – is related only through summary of changes he has passed through and by means of confrontations between him and other characters, all of whom are presented complete rather than allowed to grow through the action. As the novels proceed it becomes clear that the real structure of the action accords with an abstract scheme in which individuals represent forces or qualities which have to be manipulated by means of intrigue, melodrama and forced incident. As a representation of the actual texture of life, which it purports to be, it gives the impression of having issued prematurely through the unfortunate fluency and glibness of a writer who, for all his articulateness and intelligence, never understood the nature of the task he had set himself.

Not long after *Alice* Lytton produced one of his most successful works – *Zanoni* (1842), a strange, exotic fiction, part allegory, part fantasy, in which he directly dramatises his analysis of man. *Zanoni* departs entirely from realism and takes the line which Godwin had struck out in *St Leon* (1799). Its hero is master of a Rosicrucian cult whose initiates purchase superhuman powers and eternal life at the cost of sacrificing their emotions. Zanoni falls in love and chooses to abandon his immunity from the evils of humanity in order to love the girl who attracts him. He dies during the French Revolution in a similar situation to the hero of *A Tale of Two Cities*. The scenes which deal with the Revolution and the Terror are bizarre and fascinating. The work as a whole moves quickly and, according to its own laws, coherently. A similar success is achieved in one later novel, *A Strange Story*, where Lytton again chose a supernatural subject and allowed his imagination full scope. Here, where melodrama, romantic incident, abrupt transitions and extreme confrontations are appropriate, he succeeds. By contrast, we notice his dismal failure when he tried to respond to what he felt was the increasing demand for realist fiction and for studies of character. His *The Caxtons: A Family Picture* has what he calls 'an interior meaning' well in line with the novels of his more successful contemporaries; 'that, whatever our wanderings, our happiness will always be found within a narrow compass, and amidst the objects more immediately within our reach.'[17] But never did author more misconstrue the methods by which his aim was to be achieved. His 'Family Picture' groans and creaks its way through forced dialogue, dreary humour, tortured action and strained and maudlin sentiment, a still-born embodiment of what is implied in the most derogatory application of the term Victorian.

6 Rationalism and Real Life: the Fiction of Harriet Martineau

Harriet Martineau was brought up in Norwich in a strongly religious family, which also produced, in her younger brother James, an influential theologian and intellectual. She came from a city and a class which had been producing prominent men and women, like William Taylor and Lucy Aitkin, for some time. Originally of Huguenot stock, her family were involved in medicine and manufacture. From this point of view Martineau was typical of many Victorian intellectuals who came from newly established professional families, or from those only on the periphery of established social groups. But from another point of view she was extremely unusual – as an enthusiastic proponent of psychological materialism and political economy, to which mid-Victorian poets and novelists were strongly opposed. Because of this she made a distinctive contribution to the development of English fiction in the 1830s. As a rationalist, she was insensitive to Romantic ideas about the unity of spirit and matter, but approached the Romantic idea of organic structure in fiction from her own angle. Her religious conviction committed her to a belief that life was meaningful while her rationalism stressed the working of physical law against moral and spiritual freedom. The result was that she fixed her attention on individual and social experience as the media through which meaning could be understood and conveyed, and gradually came to the task of representing them as meaningfully related. She fell short of complete success and soon became dissatisfied with the compromise she had worked out, but at one time, in her novel *Deerbrook* (1839), she produced a striking anticipation of the characteristic features of mid-Victorian Realist fiction.

In her approach to the novel Martineau was helped a good deal by what she learned from Sir Walter Scott. From him she absorbed the idea that fiction could embody the 'whole region of moral science, politics, political economy, social rights and duties'.[1] The Waverley novels also taught her how to combine the Realism of enlightenment historians and satirists with a firm assertion of emotional and moral values. The Realism, kindliness and cheerfulness which inspired Scott's wide-ranging scenes of human life gave his work a quality which, she said, 'exhilarates the spirits and animates the affections', making it 'a great work of incitement and amelioration'.[2] She also learnt from him that fiction was potentially a great agent of morals and philosophy. Rejecting his own statements about the unimportance of fiction, she wrote: 'We rather learn from him how much may be impressed by exemplification which would be rejected in the form of reasoning, and how there may be more extensive *embodiments* of truth in fiction than the world was before thoroughly aware of.'[3]

This view was only partially realised in Martineau's earliest fiction, but even there she showed great originality. Following her discovery of the working of the laws of causality in life as a whole, she progressed logically to an enthusiastic adoption of the principles of political economy. She saw the dissemination of these principles as the most urgent task of the age and determined against great discouragement to illustrate them in fiction. As one of her biographers explains:

She thought she had discovered the great laws of nature in the principles of Smith, Ricardo, Malthus, and other contemporary Utilitarian writers. From these writers she deduced the consequences as she thought they should work out in everyday life. She attempted to find stories that would prove that the said consequences did follow from the principles she had laid down. In all this she believed she was following the scientific and mathematical interpretation of Nature, which was verified by the experience of life.[4]

John Stuart Mill and Thomas Carlyle both despised Martineau's over-simple theory,[5] and the modern reader will often yawn at her illustrations of it. Her tales often suffer from shallow research and hasty composition. They are blotched with digressions, unassimilated debate, forced conclusions, loose ends, unexplained action and obscure motivation. But they also embody a view of human life which was revolutionary then and even now remains impressive. Martineau's 'Illustrations' treat with absolute seriousness the representation of the labouring classes and especially their ordinary working life.[6] They show the whole range of social relations and the interplay between classes and individuals in social life. The effect is that the Illustrations of an inhumane theory show man with a new sense of equality and understanding – gentleman and labourer, tradesman and manufacturer, experience the same emotions, are equally affected by their mutual relations and mutual dependence on external circumstances. Each is trapped within his class situation, at the mercy of economic law. The lessons of political economy are valued only because they provide a way out of a situation in which economic survival and human dignity are equally at risk.

The scope of the Illustrations is very limited. They do not allow character study or the treatment of moral problems. But even before she had conceived the idea of the series of Illustrations, Martineau was developing interest in this direction. She understood the importance of Jane Austen, calling her 'the queen of novelists, the immortal creator of Anne Elliot, Mr. Knightley, and a score or two more of unrivalled intimate friends of the whole public.'[7] From Austen she derived what she called the 'principles which are the life of good fiction':

. . . that its interest lies in the revelation of the human
spirit which it affords; that this revelation can be better made,
as in real life, through the medium of small incidents than
of great events . . . in short, that character is a far more
important part of fiction than incident; so that incidents
derive all their value from characters while almost any series
of incidents will serve for the elucidation of character.[8]

Having assimilated this lesson, she tried to go beyond Austen
in her study of the joint effects of temperament and training on
moral character. The early story in which she tried to do this
– *Five Years of Youth, or Sense and Sentiment* – fell very far
short of permanent interest. Its design is basically faulty and
its characterisation inept. But it clearly shows the lines along
which Martineau was working – adapting Austen's techniques
until, as Mary Shelley put it, she could use them to embody
'higher philosophical views'.[9]

Before she could do this satisfactorily, in a full-length novel,
Martineau had to work out an integrated view of life. For her,
this meant solving the theological difficulties which arose from
the working of law – expressed as Divine Prescience – and
human responsibility. The solution came when she adopted the
necessarianism of the Unitarian Joseph Priestley. According to
Priestley all human actions are caused by circumstances outside
the control of the individual; what the will is at any moment is
itself 'caused' by the factors which have conditioned the
character of the individual. But the freedom of the individual
remains, at any given moment, because there is nothing inhibit-
ing choice. His ignorance of the future obliges him to act as if
he were completely free. Priestley illustrated his point by referring to the situation of a father who sees his child in danger of
drowning:

If I see my child struggling for life in the water, it is impossible I should refrain from endeavouring to save him, unless
the life of my child should suddenly become indifferent to
me, or I should percieve that all my endeavours could avail

nothing to relieve him. I cannot conceive how any specula-
tions about the event being *previously certain,* one way or
the other, should influence my conduct, so long as that
certainty is unknown to me.[10]

The philosophy which Priestley and Martineau derived from this
view placed great emphasis on intellectual enlightenment,
According to necessarianism, nothing could be done to alter
the past or the present, which the individual must cheerfully
accept, on the understanding that his own character and actions
have contributed to it. But the future could be the subject of
careful thought and self-preparation on the part of the individual and on the part of society as a whole. As Martineau
developed it, necessarianism provided a basis for great optimism
about the future of the human race. Progress was inevitable
given the degree of enlightened understanding already in existence. It also enabled her to interpret individual life meaningfully and at the same time relate it to an analysis of society at
any given time.

In *Deerbrook* Martineau planned a work based on necessarian views – an extended picture of contemporary life which
would show the relations between the laws governing psychology and social structure and which would heighten individual awareness and point the way towards freedom and moral
elevation. The novel shows life as a complex network of cause
and effect in which, given a view-point sufficiently enlightened,
moral, social, and economic factors can be seen contributing to
a meaningful whole. The title is a clue to this purpose, referring
to a geographical, social and historical entity, rather than to
an individual or a situation.[11]

Deerbrook contains three distinct elements. There is firstly
the representation of village life, which has won repeated praise
for its clarity and faithfulness; and secondly, the action concerning the Ibbotson sisters and Edward Hope, all three
strangers to the village. These two elements are clearly connected by virtue of the fact that what happens to the central

characters arises directly from the state of mind of the people they come amongst. The rivalry between the Grey and Rowland families is intensified by the appearance of the sisters, cousins of the Greys. Mrs Rowland, small-minded but strong-willed and spiteful, is exasperated by the fact that the popular Doctor Hope, in marrying Hester Ibbotson, adopts the Grey connection and is further irritated by her brother Philip's affection for Margaret. She sets gossip afoot which affects the domestic peace of the Hopes and harms his practice and also intervenes between Philip and Margaret Ibbotson. Mrs Rowland, as Hope explains, through her lack of enlightenment and moral elevation, becomes the victim of her own character and her social environment:

> 'Her hatred to us is the result of long habit of ill will, of selfish pride, and of low pertinacity about small objects. That is the way in which I account for it all . . . I take hers to be no uncommon case. The dislikes of low and selfish minds generally bear very much the character of hers, though they may not be pampered by circumstances into such a luxuriance as in this case. In a city, Mrs. Rowland might have been an ordinary spiteful fine lady. In such a place as Deerbrook, and with a family of rivals' cousins incessantly before her eyes, to exercise her passions upon, she has ended in being . . .' 'what she is,' said Margaret, as Hope stopped for a word.[12]

Hope himself, with his wife and sister-in-law, rises above all the difficulties which Mrs Rowland throws in their way because he has the qualities which she lacks. He can see the essential triviality and insignificance of his own suffering and escape from it by taking pleasure in the positive happiness he possesses in his personal relationships, and by giving thought to the inevitability of the ultimate victory of his principles.

The third element – Martineau's representation of social unrest – is less easily connected with the personal action and the study of moral contrast and development, but has often been singled out for special praise. The depiction of the effects of dearth on a hard-pressed peasant community is striking. The scene in which Margaret and Maria have to deal with a potentially violent burglary, face to face with the disguised labourer who has broken into the house at night, was selected for comment by several contemporaries. The scenes in the cottage of the same labourer when he and his wife and child are struck down by the fever, are unprecedented for their convincing realism. They leave the reader with a sharp sense of social insecurity and a strong impression of the conditions of life in the disturbed years of the third and fourth decades of the last century. Critics have attacked these sections of the novel, however, because they thought that Martineau had included them merely for their own interest, and many readers have objected particularly strongly to the use she makes of the epidemic which strikes the village. But such criticisms result from a failure to appreciate the full complexity of the author's purpose. Martineau took great care with the social background to her story and fixed the action carefully in the immediate past. The disturbances in the agricultural area around Deerbrook, the political trouble which follows Hope's firm-minded vote for a liberal candidate against the wishes of the local landowner, and the epidemic, all point to a crucial date in the period leading up to the Reform Act of 1832. The epidemic itself, referred to by one writer as a 'devastating plague lightly stirred in towards the conclusion'[18] must be identified with the national cholera epidemic of that year. The reason for this explicitness, and for the fact that Martineau extends the action beyond what arises out of the purely personal situation at all, is because she wished to stress the connection between the moral and the social effects of the dismal lack of enlightment among the village people. It was, after all, as Martineau knew as well as her doctor hero, ignorance that created the conditions in which cholera flourished, and superstition which inhibited attempts to control it. Hope himself realised that it was apt that he should become the victim of a small-minded and ignorant but powerful woman

and the object of hatred to a resentful, disturbed and super-
stitious peasantry who had been led to believe him guilty of
body-snatching. It is also apt that Mrs Rowland, through a
wrong-headed refusal to withdraw her family from the village,
invites infection into her own house and, reacting irrationally,
sends for Hope, begs him to save the child who is affected and
attempts to ward off disease by confessing the way in which she
has tried to harm him and Margaret. Hope's reflection reminds
us of the way in which every aspect of the novel is pervaded by
the moral view which he embodies:

> 'How alike is the superstition of the ignorant and the wicked!
> My poor neighbours stealing to the conjuror's tent in the
> lane, and this wretched lady, hope alike to bribe Heaven in
> their extremity . . .'[14]

As a result of Mrs Rowland's confession her brother Philip and
Margaret marry and leave Deerbrook, bringing the action of
the novel to an end. The happy ending is possible not simply
because of the confession, however, but because of the patience
and confidence the lovers have acquired through a slow process
of learning recorded in the novel. Their marriage completes the
plot and coincides with the end of a process of crisis and
development which has been taking place in Deerbrook society
at large, which has come to see the social and political need for
the qualities they possess.

An account of Martineau's artistic purpose, however, which
so clearly anticipates the work of George Eliot, might obscure
the aesthetic failure which results from her large-scale defects
of plotting and construction. These spring from her inability to
make what would have been the revolutionary step of founding
her action on internal processes of character development, as
Eliot later did. Aware of her own weakness, Martineau went to
real life for her action, basing the novel on the idea of a man
whose sense of duty obliged him to marry the sister of the
woman he actually loves because he is told that she loves him.
This is combined with the idea of two sisters of contrasting tem-

D

perament, taken over from *Five Years of Youth*. So the central predicament involves Edward Hope, who is married to Hester Ibbotson (beautiful but irritable) and her sister Margaret (plainer, but patient and strong-minded). This three-cornered relationship has the disadvantage of containing two centres of interest, provided by the character of Hester and the cruel dilemma of Hope, neither of which is very well developed. In the first instance a problem is created by the character of the doctor, whose frankness and stability are such that a fall from his horse and a severe concussion are needed to prevent him proposing to Margaret before he can be informed that Hester loves him. This incident is also used quite skilfully to make Hester aware of her own feelings and to enable Mrs Gray, the interfering matchmaker, to guess them too. When Hope recovers we transfer our attention back to him and to the dilemma Mrs Grey presents him with. Once he has decided to propose to Hester the action moves forward so as to allow us to see his problem in connection with hers, but they remain essentially distinct problems. They also prove very difficult to develop through the action which follows. Hope's own development is virtually over when he marries Hester; the fact that he comes to love her, rather than Margaret, in the course of time is more in the nature of a bonus paid out by the novelist for exceptional merit than a necessary result of his own efforts. And Hester's process of character-change has to wait for the deterioration in the external circumstances of the family before it begins, and even then has to be postponed on account of the external events which impinge on their lives. In both cases Martineau fails to dramatise any process of change, or, in fact, to create any steady development of interest.

The situation is further complicated and weakened by the way in which Martineau develops the relationship between Philip Enderby and Margaret, which has to be made a source of suffering from which Margaret can acquire philosophy and a firm scale of values. In order to retard the movement towards an obvious conclusion, Martineau invents an episode which spoils the characterisation of Philip. Mrs Rowland, determined to split up Margaret and Philip, spitefully combines truth and total falsehood and tells him that Hope and Margaret had loved each other before his marriage to Hester. This lie, which disturbs Philip beyond the comprehension of even contemporary readers, remains uncontroverted because Margaret is never given a chance to deny it. When Philip hears it he confronts Hope: the brother-in-law, unable to make a complete denial, protects Margaret from hearing the reason for Philip's abandonment of her because he thinks it is impossible to admit how far the allegation is true on his part. She writes to Philip demanding to know the reason and declaring her innocence of any fault, but the letter is intercepted and burnt by Mrs Rowland. Consequently Philip takes his grief and disillusionment back to London and Margaret remains in Deerbrook to suffer.

In spite of these large-scale deficiencies, however, the novel as a whole is effectively put together from a mechanical point of view and the undoubted success of some parts is quite well able to compensate for glaring weaknesses. So we may well imagine that if Martineau had gone on writing fiction she might well have learned to overcome her problems of plotting and construction, just as Mrs Gaskell learnt to overcome hers after *Mary Barton* and *North and South*. But her one attempt at serious fiction after *Deerbrook*, the unfinished *Oliver Weld*, appears to have been a novel of debate rather than a representation of social life. such as she had previously written, and it was very soon destroyed.[15] Her failure to develop as a novelist was actually inevitable, resulting from the same intellectual factors which made *Deerbrook* defective. The work of later novelists, similar to *Deerbrook* in many respects, rested on a firm and positive reconciliation .of psychological and social realism with moral and spiritual values. The apparent reconciliation embodied in *Deerbrook* was factitious, consisting in nothing more than a temporary balance in Martineau's mind of elements which were bound to separate out.

Growing awareness of man as determined by environment and history, and increasing confidence in the habits of analysis, led Martineau eventually to scepticism. And with her loss of faith in the spiritual dimension of experience went her belief in the possibility of finding meaning within human life. She simply ceased to think that man was at the centre of meaning, or, as she put it herself, came to realise the full implications of Copernicanism. So she turned away from religion and literature and found consolation in the beliefs afforded by mesmerism. She came to think that adjustment to the vital principle whose working seemed evident in mesmerism was the sole means of giving significance to human life – that 'philosophy founded upon science is the one thing needful, – the source and vital principle of all intellectuality, all morality, and all peace to individuals, and goodwill among men'.[16] She abandoned the novel even before the outburst of realist fiction in the later 1840s, and the years which saw the publication of the major works of Dickens, Thackeray, Charlotte Brontë, George Eliot and George Meredith, saw her preoccupied with the task of identifying the scientific laws affecting man's development. At this distance, the view of wiser contemporaries is justified and she seems childishly naïve. But this last phase was only the end of a process which had, in its course, been productive of more convincing attitudes. In earlier years the necessarian compromise had enabled her to hold in solution more than rationalist elements and so to create a mode of fiction which is original, historically important and also of permanent interest.

7 Frederick Denison Maurice, Romantic, Christian, Victorian

F. D. Maurice made his mark on Victorian England as a theologian, an educationalist and a social critic, but the impact of his work went far beyond the barriers these categories imply. His importance derives from the fact that he was among the first Victorian writers to reach a point from which, as H. G. Wood has put it, 'he could defend freedom of enquiry in the study of both history and nature and where he could welcome the results of such enquiry because his faith rested on another foundation than the traditional authority of Church or Bible.'[1] The confidence and courage with which Maurice worked to reconcile Romantic truth with rationalist enquiry made his work valuable to many who did not share his Christianity. For them he provided a pattern within which the ever-growing humanist insistence on the importance of human experience could he reconciled with established social and political institutions and given moral and spiritual content. His career marks an important stage in the process by which Romantic ideas were modified to form the basis of the Victorian novel. Maurice saw himself as the immediate heir of the English Romantic poets and a representative of the revolution in European thought and feeling, by which materialist thought had begun to give way to a new idealism. This revolution, he thought, was 'quite as signal as that which distinguished the middle of the seventeenth century, though of a directly opposite kind'.[2] It involved three separate factors: the abandonment of mechanical and materialist conceptions of man's nature; insistence on the integrity of his experience; and construction of a new perspective in intellectual and spiritual affairs:

> It does not consist in any dry, tame, acknowledgement that man has an important part or property which may survive the dissolution of his animal frame; it amounts to nothing less than a distinct affirmation, that those powers and properties which he has within him, of which the senses can take no account, and which are not reducible under any mechanical conditions, are what constitute him a man; and that all the most important part of his history is the history of these powers, of the restraints to which they have been subjected and of what they have achieved.[3]

Maurice traced this revolution through the work of Kant, and into the English Methodist movement. He found different aspects of it in the work of Wordsworth, Byron and Shelley, and recognised Walter Scott as a representative of one of its central aspects. He praised Scott's humanity and fertility and connected him with Wordsworth as an advocate of 'the great truth which was hidden' under all the wildness of the French Revolution, 'and which sober Englishmen could turn to the best account, that there is a priceless grandeur in every human being, and that neither literature nor society can exist unless they confess that grandeur and seek to awaken the sense of it.[4] But he also thought that Scott was insensitive to the changes which had come about in awareness of the internal life of man and the forces at work in contemporary society. His criticism precedes the similar attacks of Carlyle and Martineau:

> He has seen the outward, but he has not connected it with that which is within. He has looked at the conduct, and listened to the speech, of men, but he has not understood from what kind of central source their deeds and words are drawn. . . . In his dialogues, he in some degree gets over the

difficulty, by repartees, passion, and mimicry of the language of the time; but in soliloquies, how barren and incomplete appears to be his psychology! and compare these, or even the best parts of the conversations, with a scene of Shakespeare, and the difference may at once be perceived between writers, the one of whom knows nothing but phenomena, while the other, with to the full as much of individual observation, was also imbued with the largest abundance that any man ever had of universal truth.[5]

Maurice owed a great deal to Scott, and to the other English and German Romantics, especially to Coleridge, but he saw the need for something like the modern distinction between Romantic and Victorian. He thought that the deepest concern of the previous generation had been subjective, whereas in his own generation there was need for a social and objective validation of the central spiritual affirmation. The publication of Wordsworth's *Prelude* drew from him a perceptive comment on its representative value:

. . . Wordsworth's Prelude seems to me the dying utterance of the half-century we have just passed through, the expression – the English expression at least – of all that self-building process in which, according to their different schemes and principles, Byron, Goethe, Wordsworth, the Evangelicals (Protestant and Romantist) were all engaged, which their novels, poems, experiences, prayers, were setting forth, in which God, under whatever name, or in whatever aspect he presented Himself to them, was still the agent only in fitting them to be world-wise, men of genius, artists, saints. For us there must be something else intended – either the mere science millenium of Comte, from which good Lord deliver us, or the knowledge and life of God as the ground of all human and earthly knowledge and life.[6]

Beneath the Christian terminology of this statement lies Maurice's fundamental belief that it is the task of his own generation to work towards a vision of contemporary life in all its aspects as an organic unity, infused with spiritual meaning.

Of all the earlier Romantic writers, it seemed to Maurice that it was Coleridge who had been the most immediately useful to those who followed him. In his rambling, unsystematic way, but according to Maurice his essentially practical and pragmatic way too, Coleridge had tackled the central problem of applying Romantic ideas to the immediate circumstances of English life. So far as religion was concerned Maurice had learnt from Coleridge 'the inward witness which a gospel of facts possesses and which a gospel of notions must always want – how the most awful and absolute truths, which notions displace or obscure, are involved in facts, and through facts may be entertained and embraced . . .'[7] From this point he went on to understand the importance of the intellectual techniques which permit the accurate identification and description of facts as distinct from the pseudo-facts, mere notions, or forms. Consequently, he came to believe it was imperative that the modern thinker reconcile the two conflicting principles which J. S. Mill identified as Benthamite analysis and Coleridgean appreciation of the elements of continuity and relatedness in experience.[8] Mill's description of these principles drew from Maurice a statement of his own view of the task which confronted the Victorian intellectual:

> Coleridge belonged to another generation than ours – one of which the business was to indicate the preciousness of truths as distinct from facts. This function he performed marvellously well. It is wrong to disparage either him or the matter-of-fact men of the last century. So far as either did his work right, he caught occasional glimpses of the principle realised by the other, sufficient to hinder him from walking in darkness. But I believe also that we are come upon an age in which truth without facts will be as impossible as facts without truth: and that the attempt to set up either exclusively

must be conducted on quite a different spirit from that which animated Coleridge or the good men of the preceding age, however the result may at times correspond.[9]

Rationalism had attacked and destroyed the empty notions of eighteenth century orthodoxy, substituting the facts of psychology and nature. The Romantic revolution had asserted the primacy of spiritual truth over the purely material dimension with which rationalists had been concerned. Maurice's own task, he thought, was to assert that only through facts which rationalist processes established could truth be apprehended at all by humankind.

Once he had arrived at this position Maurice spent the rest of his life as an active propagandist of his own views and, as a practical reformer, trying to put them into practice. But part of his importance lies in the fact that he was only the most articulate and aggressive representative of a large and important group of artists and intellectuals who shared the same fundamental attitudes. In Cambridge he had been the leading spirit among a brilliant group of students who shared a community of thought and feeling and which later broke up to disseminate their ideas throughout Victorian society. Among these 'apostles' Maurice found many friends who were later to become leading figures in English life, and all of whom shared the devotion to Romantic principles and his openness to rationalist and reformist ideas. As one of their number described them later in life, with a mixture of condescension and nostalgia, the ideas of the group were quite clear:

We held established principles, especially in poetry and metaphysics, and set up certain idols for our worship. Coleridge and Wordsworth were our principal divinities, and Hare and Thirlwall were regarded as their prophets: or rather in the celestial hierarchy I should have put Shakespeare at the top of all, and I should have found a lofty pedestal for Kant and Goethe. It was with a vague idea that it should be our function to interpret the oracles of transcendental wisdom to the

D*

world of Philistines, or Stumpfs, as we designated them, and
from time to time to call forth from this world a few souls
who might be found capable of sympathizing with them, that
we piqued ourselves on the name of the 'Apostles' – a name
given us, as we were sometimes told by the envious and jeer-
ing vulgar, but to which we presumed that had a legiti-
mate claim, and gladly accepted it.[10]

When Maurice left Cambridge, with his brilliant friend John
Sterling, it was to propagate the ideas of the apostles in London,
among Utilitarians, Radicals and Conservatives, in the London
Debating Club, and through the columns of the *Athenaeum*.
They had to give up the *Athenaeum* after a year or so, but
while they held it, they made it the vehicle of an attack on the
philistinism of Whigs and Tories alike, and on the party spirit
in politics and journalism. In the *Athenaeum* Romantic literature found sympathetic but objective explication, and the fore-
most ideas of the age were examined on their own merits. At
the same time, however, dissatisfied with a merely critical function, Maurice began to integrate the ideas he derived from
literature with his view of contemporary society and with the
religious conceptions which were coming to dominate his life.
In doing this he turned towards the novel as the apt medium
for the process of exposition and discovery. The resulting work,
Eustace Conway, The Brother and Sister, a Novel, was written
and re-written at intervals between 1826 and 1833. It is at the
same time one of the most revealing and one of the worst of the
novels of the period. It is extremely interesting because it
attempts to embody a coherent view of contemporary life in its
social, political and intellectual aspects and tries to bring them
together dramatically. The central ideas which Maurice develops
in the novel are an early version of those which feature in the
novels of his successors. The central character, Eustace, begins
life as an enthusiastic Utilitarian, but quickly loses his naïve
hope of reforming the world and the nature of man, and with
it loses his morals, his faith in life, his confidence, and sense of

purpose. He also drifts away from his sister Honoria, who is distinguished from her brother by the unreflecting faith and good nature which save her from wordly temptation but make her susceptible to another kind of evil influence from a selfish, power-loving female friend, and a passionate, tormented, lover. Some way through the second volume, Eustace meets a German *émigré* who converts him to a belief in the reality of the spiritual dimension of life. Under this influence Eustace shakes off his aimlessness, escapes from the 'evil spirit of refinement which would destroy the action under pretence of purifying the motive'[11] and is able to believe again in the possibility of improving human life by refining the character. His development is completed by an English clergyman who brings him round to Christianity by making him realise the nature of the desires implanted in human nature:

> . . . even the universal denial which barricades every avenue through which doubt may enter in, has found no artifice for excluding the question 'What am I?' It came to me again, and again and again. Physical science, I knew could not answer it – no, not even Fichte, with his *Ich*, and his *Nicht, Jah*. Poetry could not answer it: for, though it embodies all the operations of self, that mighty agent it can never discover. Nor should I ever have found an answer to it, if I had not learnt the meaning of that voice which the Jewish shepherd heard at night proclaiming from a burning bush – 'I AM THAT I AM!'[12]

With his faith confirmed by his sister's example of patience amidst severe suffering, Eustace ends happily, married to a cousin and firmly settled in English society. Other characters end less well. Passionate Francisca, half Irish, half Spanish, sins repeatedly through excess of passion and impulsiveness, murders her lover and drowns herself. Utilitarian Rumbolt tries to abduct a wealthy Quakeress and escapes to the Continent, shifting the blame temporarily to Eustace. Mrs Hartenfeld, selfish and insidious in her attempts to dominate those around her, is

detected in immorality, obliged to disgorge ill-gotten gains, and
dies mysteriously. Honoria also dies, worn down by abrasive
contact with a rough world. Fortunately Eustace's brother and
his wife live happily on, blessed with a baby, to compensate
for some years of misery and distress.

Eustace Conway contains no central action, but shifts in-
coherently between three intrigues, all of which are mechani-
cally connected through letters, disclosures, confessions and
amazing events. The characterisation is lamentable, the construction impossible, and the modern reader – if he finishes the
novel at all – will find it obscure and disjointed. On the other
hand, it deeply impressed J. S. Mill and interested Coleridge. It
is still interesting as an indication of the themes and problems typical of the period from the later 1820s when more than
one writer struggled unsuccessfully to twist the novel into a shape
which could embody a serious analysis of contemporary problems and a coherent, wide-ranging, analysis of life. The leading
characteristics of *Eustace Conway* are shared by novels like J.
Lockhart's *Reginald Dalton*, John Sterling's *Arthur Coningsby*
and even the early fiction of G. H. Lewes.[13] All these writers
sensed that the novel was a literary form most appropriate to
their purpose of reconciling Romantic values with social
criticism in an organic view of life, but none of them were able
to shape their fiction from natural events. Instead they give the
impression of patching and cobbling as they go along, seeking
through mechanical devices the confidence and coherent vision
which later novelists seem to possess as their natural right.

After the publication of *Eustace Conway*, Maurice turned
away from fiction. Around the same time he gave up the
Athenaeum and returned to university – this time at Oxford –
to finish his degree. After Oxford came ordination as an
Anglican priest, marking his abandonment of his father's
Unitarianism and his new conviction that spiritual truth had
to be presented through concrete institutions. Shortly after-
wards he published a volume which contains the outline of all
his later writings and shows him irretrievably committed to

a directness of thought and expression which made the novel an inappropriate form. This book, *The Kingdom of Christ* (1838), covers the whole intellectual range of the period, connecting political, social, economic, and literary developments of the previous half-century in one coherent view. Here Maurice formulated strong yet flexible criteria which could be made to validate his central religious convictions and be applied directly to contemporary situations. He argues in *The Kingdom of Christ* that while the religious ideas discovered and established since the Reformation were 'solid and imperishable', the systems created to embody them were approaching dissolution. He identified these ideas as: insistence on the spirituality of man, derived from Quakerism: the actuality of Christ's incarnation, embodied in Lutheranism: and, from Unitarianism, 'belief in the unity of God, the absolute love of God, the existence of a good and pure state for mankind'.[14] The question of how these ideas should be maintained as religious principles outside of any particular system in which they had previously existed, was capable of solution, Maurice thought, only if another principle were taken up. This further principle had been strongly held by the Quakers but had been a permanent element in human thought and was actually growing stronger in the modern world – that there existed, or should exist, a universal spiritual kingdom of which all men were members by virtue of their humanity. In the eighteenth century the dominance of materialist psychology and the denial of man's spiritual nature had led to the modification of this idea to that 'of a very comprehensive *world*, which should include all nations, systems, religions', and it was this idea that was embodied in the French Revolution.[15] It was followed by the spiritual awakening in Europe as a whole, which resulted in 'a greater value for personal religion', a desire among men to combine for spiritual objects, and the renewing of the question of whether the fellowship of man might not have a spiritual foundation.

Maurice associated this development with the parallel movement in philosophy and literature and the tendency to look on man 'as essentially a spiritual creature'.[16] He connected it also with the eager and passionate demands among working men 'for a universal constitution into which men as men might enter',[17] and saw this as similar to the impulse which produced Utilitarianism, St Simonianism and Owenite Socialism. Maurice's most original quality was that he was able to appreciate these parallels, not merely using them for the sake of his own argument, but taking them as support for the conclusion that the spiritual kingdom of which man is a member must be identified with the physical world in which he lives – 'that the spiritual and universal society must be involved in the very idea of our human constitution, say rather, must be that constitution, by virtue of which men realise that there is a humanity, that we form a kind.'[18]

Maurice found further evidence for this spiritual constitution in the existence of families and nations, which were for him types of the greater union, which, like them, had abstract and concrete existence. He also detected within Christianity in general certain Catholic institutions and events pointing towards the universality and reality of the faith itself: baptism, the creeds, forms of worship, the eucharist, the ministerial orders and the scriptures. Because of the nature of English society and English character, he argued that the spiritual and universal brotherhood could not exist in England apart from existing institutions and especially the English Church. But the English Church could only represent the universal Church so long as it furthered the principles which underlay it, rather than the systems or parties of those who tried to identify it with their special dogmas. Above all, Maurice thought, it was important that the Church should work so as to encourage human unity by stressing the unity between Christ and man, as King and subject of a spiritual kingdom which the individual entered through baptism, by right of his humanity. In normal times and places the role of the true Christian churchman would be to encourage true elements in the religion of others outside his own church. Typically, however, Maurice gave a special role to those who worked in disturbed industrial districts, where the priorities of ordinary men were often aggressively non-spiritual. Here Maurice would proclaim, to the Chartist and the Socialist, that 'God has cared for you, you are indeed his children . . . There is a fellowship larger, more irrespective of outward distinctions, more democratical, than any which you can create . . .'[19] But he would continue in words which formed the germ of his late political and religious creed and provided the starting point of the Christian Socialist Movement: 'But it is a fellowship of mutual love, not mutual selfishness, in which the chief is the servant of all.'[20]

The Kingdom of Christ embodied Maurice's deepest convictions about the actual brotherhood of man, its spiritual basis and its confirmation in the person of Christ. From these convictions stemmed activities which struck to the heart of problems central to Victorian life. In his own day Maurice found more opponents than disciples. His theology seemed obscure and heretical to Christians; and many rationalists found his thinking irredeemably vague and confused. But his work had immediate and substantial impact on his generation. It was the main channel by which the forces at work in early Victorian culture were brought home to a wider public in practical life than was reached by writers less concerned with social and religious reform. Maurice turned attention to the spiritual or non-material dimension of human character, and showed that it formed part of a meaningful whole, with the laws governing economic and social existence. He gave the example of a unified view of life, showed the way its elements could be brought together, and created, even in minds that did not accept his religious premises, a priority which later found concrete embodiment in the novel. Like others in the 1820s and 1830s, he failed to master the novel himself, but his achievement in theology and criticism helped greatly to mould the sensibility of which the novel was to prove the most appropriate form of expression.

8 Thomas Carlyle, Prophet of the Real

The importance of Carlyle's writing was well understood during his own lifetime. As George Eliot remarked, in 1855, when Carlyle was in his sixtieth year: 'there is hardly a superior or active mind of this generation that has not been modified by Carlyle's writings; there has hardly been an English book written for the last ten or twelve years that would not have been different if Carlyle had not lived.'[1] This influence derived ultimately from Carlyle's ability as a literary artist, but more directly it resulted from the fact that he was able to offer a satisfying cure for contemporary intellectual and moral ailments. His creed rested on the assertion that man was a spiritual and social being, and that his life could be meaningful only so long as he sought integration and self-fulfilment, rather than self-indulgence. Carlyle taught that the first step to maturity and understanding was the acceptance of the real, leading eventually to the 'open secret' of life – that the ideal is immanent in the real, the supernatural in the natural. He showed how the trivial and sordid, limiting, circumstances of human existence are the medium through which sublimity and significance exist. And – most important of all for the history of literature – he introduced his contemporaries to the idea that it was the special function of literature to express this view of life. He accepted something very close to the Coleridgean view of the imagination and described the imagination's product as at once an embodiment of reality and an organic poem. There were many channels by which these ideas flowed into the main current of Victorian thinking, but of them all, Carlyle's was the most persuasively argued and seemed the most directly relevant. His writings are an integral part of the development of Realism.

It is interesting to compare Carlyle with his exact contemporary, Keats. Some of their ideas are very similar – their anti-materialism and anti-rationalism, for example, are part of the general body of Romantic thought. But whereas Keats, at a surprisingly early age, had been able to assimilate the central Romantic ideas from his predecessors and contemporaries and to begin to relate them to contemporary social and philosophical problems immediately, it took Carlyle very much longer and then was the reward of hard and sustained study. Carlyle, in fact, could not gain from Romantic poetry as Keats had done. Wordsworth meant little to him, Shelley less. He respected Coleridge to a certain extent, but despised his lack of will and his preoccupation with Anglican theology and German metaphysics. Byron earned more wholehearted respect, but only for his negative critical achievement in attacking hypocrisy and for the energy with which he expressed the sensitive soul's dissatisfaction with the world. As a young man Carlyle had shared this discontent. Educated by his Calvinist parents for the Church, he had lost his religious faith by his twentieth year and wandered for several subsequent years in a desert – a world deprived of meaning or comfort.

It was presumably because of his philosophical and theological training, and perhaps because of the qualities inherited from his Calvinist parents, that Carlyle had been unable to find a way out of this burnt and blackened waste of scepticism through poetry. He had to wander further afield until he came into contact with the work of Goethe and his German contemporaries. Shortly after this he experienced a mystical conversion, a convulsion of feeling, which formed the basis of the later conversion of his philosopher-hero in *Sartor Resartus*. Kant and Goethe, as he

understood them, gave him a means of escaping from the position into which French and Scottish materialism and scepticism
had forced him. In his early essays he propounds the Kantean
distinction between understanding and reason as the basis of
a view of life in which the positive elements of criticism and
science could co-exist with a renewed religious faith. The sphere
of understanding is 'practical and material knowledge', where
it is 'the strength and universal implement of the mind'. Reason
does not work 'by logic or argument', but in the higher region,
'whither logic and argument cannot reach':

> . . . in that holier region, where Poetry and Virtue and
> Divinity abide, in whose presence Understanding wavers and
> recoils, dazzled into utter darkness by that 'sea of light', at
> once the fountain and the termination of all true knowledge.[2]

So Kantean reason enabled the thinker to see beyond the
separate facts marshalled by logic, to the realm beyond, where
they existed as the separate parts of a larger whole. To embody
this vision was the task of imaginative literature; the organic
nature of ultimate reality could only be figured forth in the
poem.

In this way Carlyle dignified art beyond even the degree to
which the Romantic poets had done so. He also developed some
central Romantic ideas further than they had been previously
taken. Arguing that the function of the poem was to represent
the ordinary, so as to suggest the extraordinary, Carlyle threw
a new emphasis on the representation of immediate reality and
gave a philosophical dimension to the practical, democratic view
embodied in the novels of Scott and the *Lyrical Ballads* of
Wordsworth and Coleridge:

> The poet, we imagine, can never have far to seek for a sub-
> ject: the elements of his art are in him, and around him on
> every hand; for him the Ideal world is not remote from the
> Actual, but under it and within it: nay he is a poet, precisely
> because he can discern it there. Wherever there is a sky above

him, and a world around him, the poet is in his place, for here too is man's existence, with its infinite longings and small acquirings; its ever-thwarted and ever-renewed endeavours; its unspeakable aspirations, its fears and hopes that wander through Eternity; and all the mystery of brightness and of gloom that it was ever made of, in any age or climate, since man first began to live. Is there not the fifth act of a Tragedy in every death-bed, though it were a peasant's and a bed of heath?[3]

The work of the greatest artist, taking account of all reality, with criticism as sharp as the bitterest cynic but with a healing and harmonising spirit of love, can be described as 'truer than reality itself, since the essence of unmixed reality is bodied forth in them under more expressive symbols'.[4] To understand the process by which this came to be was the work of the critic or student of literature – to understand how, in the case of Shakespeare's plays, each work 'springs, as it were, from the general elements of all thought, and grows up therefrom, into form and expansion by its own growth'.[5]

It was as a critic that Carlyle first began to have an impact on the English reading public, showing them how antimaterialism could be combined with insistence on reality and a concern for contemporary social problems. But before this Carlyle had tried the higher function, and attempted to embody the same philosophy in fiction of his own. Over a period of years, he tried several times to write a novel, but each time with signal lack of success. This may partly be attributed to the fact that it was only after his later essays that he had the self-awareness and clarity of mind needed to produce a substantial work of art. But we have to notice also that it would have been quite impossible to do what Carlyle wanted to do with the novel at that time without a degree of imaginative originality which he never possessed. To write a novel in his early manhood Carlyle would have needed an action and a style which could dramatise a process of development; it would also have had to be capable of showing man's essentially social nature, of realising actual material conditions and of conveying the central statement concerning the immanence of the ideal in the real. Some of his attempts at this hopeless task were made before he had encountered *Wilhelm Meister,* which had gone further than any previous novel towards achieving these aims. But even after reading *Wilhelm Meister* Carlyle failed to take it as a model. Carlyle's view of life demanded greater involvement and intensity of feeling than Goethe's, and he was dissatisfied with the means by which Goethe had brought the separate parts of his fiction together.

Carlyle's first attempt at a novel is recorded in a letter to Jane Welsh, as early as October 1822. This story was to have embodied the theme he elsewhere described as central to literature itself – the clash between necessity and subjective desires:

> I would paint, in a brief but vivid manner, the old story of a noble mind struggling against an ignoble fate; some fiery yet benignant spirit reaching forth to catch the bright creations of his own fancy and breaking his head against the vulgar obstacles of the lower world: But then what know I of this lower world? The man must be a hero, and I could only draw the materials from myself. Rich source of such materials! Besides, it were well that he died of love; and your novel love is become a perfect drug; and of the genuine sort, I could not undertake to say a word.[6]

This Wertherian project laid aside, he suggested a modified plan to Jane, whereby they should write together. The new plan was for an epistolary novel about a middle-class Byron, 'entirely sick of struggling along the sordid bustle of existence, where he could glean so little enjoyment but found so much acute suffering'. He was to fly from mankind to the countryside, to meditate on nature and converse with people met by chance, on science and literature, and then, tired of the country, to lapse into bitter Byronic railing:

. . . not in the puling Lake-style – but with a tongue of fire –
sharp, sarcastic, apparently unfeeling, yet all the while be-
tokening to the quick-sighted a mind of lofty thoughts and
generous affections smarting under the torment of its own
over-nobleness, and ready to break in pieces by the force of
its own energies.[7]

At this point the Byronic hero is saved from himself by falling
in love with the heroine – her letters to be written by Miss
Welsh: 'The earth again grows green beneath his feet', but
before promised happiness can ensue, unspecified obstacles arise,
both are broken hearted and quickly die. The story was to end
with 'a company of undertakers'.[8]

Not surprisingly, Carlyle wrote only the first two letters, and
then burnt them. The story as he had conceived it would not
really have allowed him to write about the ideas and experiences which had already come to be central to his own
intellectual life. As with the earlier scheme, this was no more
than the cliché of fiction, remembered patterns of action, derived
from Goethe, Senancour or Thomas Plumer Ward. Around the
same time Carlyle did succeed in finishing one short tale, which
perhaps deserves a little more praise than it is usually given, but
which also suggests a lack of direction and uncertainty of purpose. 'Cruthers and Johnson' opens with the events leading to
a swearing of a pact of friendship between two schoolboys, and
goes on to show how it was kept up, but it lacks a coherent
purpose. The main action results from the fecklessness of one
friend, which brings his life and fortune in danger, and goes on
to show him finding a new sense of purpose and mental stability
in Jamaica, where he marries his employer's daughter, later
returning to buy back his ancestral lands. Another centre of
interest, however, exists around his imprisonment; when he is
comforted and sustained by his childhood friend. And the tale
actually ends by stressing the transitoriness of all human experience! We can only assume that the idea of the two contrasting types and the friendship which grew out of conflict,

surviving separation and difference, attracted Carlyle, but that he simply lacked, at this stage, the ability to develop it consistently.

Some four years later, after the publication of his essays on Schiller, on *Wilhelm Meister,* and on German Romance, Carlyle produced another fragment – 'Illudo Chartis'. This story shows a new influence from Sterne and John Paul Richter, and also foreshadows in matters of detail several of the features of the biography of Diogenes Teuflesdrockh. There is also more of his own biography buried here than in previous ventures. The hero is one who could say of himself; 'My whole life has been a continuous fever-dream, and my awakening will be in hell'. He suffers the agonies of his predecessors – a corroded heart, and blackened future. From what we can judge of the fragment he was to have suffered in struggling to grow beyond the limitations of his peasant environment, and perhaps a disappointment in love – scorn from a more refined and socially elevated mistress? – was in store for him. The story's most interesting aspect is its ironical method – this is Carlyle's first attempt at approaching his subject indirectly. What must strike the reader familiar with his later works, however, is that in 'Illudo Chartis' he was trying his hand at a kind of muted humour, which gave him no chance to develop his characteristic blend of dogmatic commentary, dramatic narrative and metaphysical profundity.[8]

After 'Illudo Chartis' came Carlyle's nearest success, though this, too, was left as a fragment. *Wooton Reinfred* begins with the despair of the youthful but 'interesting' hero, after he has been forbidden to see a young woman whom he loves and who he thinks has left him for someone else. Like Carlyle and Diogenes, Wooton has had a difficult childhood. Incapable of adjusting to the crude atmosphere of school, and over-influenced by his religious mother, he is sent off to college at fifteen and loses his faith:

Who knows not the agonies of doubt? What heart, not of stone, can endure to abide with them? Wooton's heart was a heart of flesh, and of the softest; it was torn and bleeding, yet he could not pause; for a voice from the depth of his nature called to him, as he loved truth, to persevere. He studied the sceptical writers of his own country; above all, the modern literature of France. Here at length a light rose upon him, not the pure sunlight of former days, but a red fierce glare, as by degrees his doubt settled in utter negation. He felt a mild pleasure mingled with his pangs, as unbelief was laying waste in scornful triumph so many fairest things, still dear and venerable even as delusions. Alas! the joy of the Denier is not of long continuance. He burns the city, and warms himself at the blaze for a day; but on the morrow the fair palaces as well as the noisome alleys are gone, and he stands houseless amid ashes and void silence. Thus also it fared with Reinfred.[9]

Wooton is fortunate at this stage of his career in attracting the attention and friendship of his cousin, Bernard Swale, whose affection distracts him from his problems and lightens his fixed melancholy. Then his meeting with Jane Montague leads to a relationship which confirms him in idealistic hopes and sublime cravings:

In her, hour after hour, a fairer and fairer soul unveiled itself; a soul of quickest vision and the gracefullest expression, so gay yet so enthusiastic, so blandishing yet so severe; a being all gentleness and fire; meek, timid, loving as the dove and high and noble as the eagle. To him her presence brought with it airs from heaven. A balmy rest encircled his spirit while near her; pale doubt fled away to the distance, and life bloomed up with happiness and hope. The young man seemed to awake as from a haggard dream; he had been in the garden of Eden, then, and his eyes could not discern it! But now the black walls of his prison melted away, and the captive was alive and free in the sunny spring![10]

When Jane breaks off the relationship on the instructions of her guardian, and for reasons unknown, Wooton is plunged back into despair. Her image is blackened and he wakes from a dream of love to a godless and dreary world.

The action up to this point is summarised at the beginning of the fragment. It actually begins after the desertion, just before Wooton is persuaded to travel with Bernard in search of distraction. The mere fact of making this decision alleviates his condition and he is helped further when he is admitted by a chance acquaintance into a charming intellectual circle. At this point the action effectively ceases and the novel opens out into a series of debates and conversations at a country house, where the guests put large-scale questions – the nature of poetry, the state of society, the possibility of happiness – under review. In these debates the idealist view, close to Carlyle's own, is given to a Coleridgean character called Dalbrook, who was probably designed to have some profound effect on the hero or to serve as a commentator on his fate. But we can only guess about how it might have developed. The debates are brought to a sudden end and Wooton rides out into the countryside, proving his sensitivity to natural beauty, where he meets Jane Montague again, in mysterious circumstances. The patient reader is just about to hear her life-story, when the fragment breaks off.

No one has lost much through this sudden termination of Wooton's story. It could only have developed along lines similar to those which wander through the novels of Maurice and Sterling. At this stage in his career, though he felt strongly drawn towards the novel as a vehicle of his developing view of life, Carlyle was completely unable to master it. In retrospect we may fancy we see that his particular view point could never be that of the novelist, because it was not with the texture of human experience he was concerned, but with a certain angle of vision, from which it could be seen as the point of contact between two modes of being, time and eternity, spirit and matter. But his failure in the novel is also typical of writers of this period in general, who shared his desire for a degree of control and certainty which fiction could not allow. Alone in the period from 1818 to 1845 he was able to create a sustained fiction in *Sartor Resartus*, but this was only when he returned to a blend of humour and irony and imposed a fantastical, satirical treatment on a straightforward narration and exposition, illuminating reality, but with a bizarre and strange light.

Carlyle began *Sartor Resartus* by working up an idea for an essay entitled 'Thoughts on Clothes'. It was under this title that the book's first version was briefly submitted for publication in November 1830 before it was rapidly reclaimed, its biographical section expanded and transformed into *Sartor Resartus*. In this final form it represents the whole range of ideas which Carlyle had worked out over the previous decade, the product of his study and meditation of French rationalism, German metaphysics, political economy and modern literature. *Sartor* is also the most coherent and positive embodiment of Carlyle's view of life, and in this respect it is significant that it works not only by humour and exaggeration, but also by indirection and repetition. It is interesting that in *Wooton Reinfred* some of his most treasured ideas are set forth not only without the narrator's authority but even under serious question by other characters. The central idea of *Sartor* is there set before the reader and left to fend for itself.

'Is not all visible nature, all sensible existence, the symbol and vesture of the Invisible and Infinite? Is it not in these material shows of things that God, virtue, immortality are shadowed forth and made manifest to man? Material nature is as a *fata-morgana*, hanging in the air; a cloud-picture, but painted by the heavenly light; in itself it is air and nothingness, but behind it is the glory of the sun. Blind men! they think the cloud-city a continuing habitation, and the sun but a picture because their eyes do not behold him. It is only the invisible that really is, but only the gifted sense can of itself discern this reality!'

'Now, in Heaven's name', cried Burridge, 'what is all this? Must a poet become a mystic, and study Kant before he can write verses? I declare, philosophers are like to turn one's brain.'[11]

In the essays which follow *Wooton Reinfred*, where Carlyle outlined his convictions about the ideality of space and time, the function of the poet, the sterility of materialism and Utilitarian morality and political economy, he did so as the exponent of other men's ideas, offering new fields of speculation to the insular English reader. Increasingly he used invented figures as mouthpieces, and quoted his own anonymous statements in support of still anonymous views. In *Sartor Resartus* this indirection takes on a new literary function.

The central idea in *Sartor Resartus* is the hero's ironic advice that we should worship clothes. Teuflesdrockh's apparent argument runs as follows: clothes make the difference between one man and another, all being born and dying naked, without the authority they confer. Power, then, lies in clothes, which denote authority and symbolise it, attracting reverence to themselves. Superficially the advocacy of this view, as the puzzled editor recognises, seems in the direction of political radicalism. But Teuflesdrockh takes care to avoid this, directing our attention rather to the fact that authority actually does work by seemingly mysterious agency among men; that human nature recognises non-material forces as factors governing conduct. Furthermore, behind the apparent irony of the clothes metaphor there is a further dimension. Clothes stand to these motivating forces as the body to the spirit. Kantean terms are brought in to reinforce this idea, establishing the unreality of matter, the reality of spirit. So the clothes philosophy of Diogenes Teuflesdrockh works in two ways at once. It asserts the weakness and insignificance of man – he is naked, a forked radish, ludicrously 'overheaped with shreds and tatters raked from the Charnel-house of Nature' – but it also elevates him to the highest position, as the arbiter of nature and the source of all meaning. The two ideas are frequently brought together in the vivid prose of Teuflesdrockh, presented to us by the fictional editor:

'. . . to the eye of vulgar Logic', says he, 'what is man? An omnivorous biped that wears Breeches. To the eye of Pure Reason what is he? A Soul, a Spirit, and divine Apparition. Round his mysterious Me, there lies, under all those wool-rags, a Garment of Flesh (or of Senses), contextured in the loom of Heaven; whereby he is revealed to his like, and dwells with them in Union and Division; and sees and fashions for himself a Universe, with azure Starry Spaces, and long Thousands of Years. Deep-hidden is he under that strange Garment; amid Sounds and Colours and Forms, as it were, swathed-in and inextricably over-shrouded: yet it is sky-woven, and worthy of a God. Stands he not thereby in the centre of Imensities, in the conflux of Externities . . . Well said Saint Chrystostom, with his lips of gold, "the true SHEKINAH is Man": where else is the GOD'S PRESENCE mani-fested not to our eyes only, but to our hearts, as in our fellow-man.'[12]

Carlyle's ultimate purpose in *Sartor Resartus* is to educate his reader so that he can experience the same vision. To this end he must simultaneously produce in him critical perception, to pierce through the forms to the inner reality, and wonder, the fit response to the reality itself. This dual aim dictates a method which will prevent the reader from consolidating his impressions at any point and from taking up a firm attitude, either towards the clothes philosophy or its originator. Consequently, Carlyle invents the editor, whose struggles to make sense of the German system attract sympathy and amusement. His presence and personality are most evident in the first section, where they serve to give Teuflesdrockh himself a context and to qualify the outrageousness of the unadulterated philosophy. In Book II where the reader learns how Teuflesdrockh came to maturity and is introduced to the biographical experiences which affected him, the editor is less necessary. In Book III he emerges again to take the responsibility of selecting passages from Teuflesdrockh's work which reflect on the social, political and religious institutions of contemporary England.

Sartor Resartus, though such an early work, marks the highest point of Carlyle's achievement in imaginative literature. From this point on he moved consistently towards history, commentary and social criticism, and as he did so tended to depreciate imaginative literature as Fiction, in contrast to history and biography, as Fact. Yet in a sense the tendency and the effect of his work remained constant. The fact that he was prepared in *Sartor Resartus* to go to the lengths of creating and then fragmenting a 'philosophy' for Teuflesdrockh indicates one of the most important features of his thinking. The strongest element in his work is the visual. He sees in flashes and makes his narration move through a series of pictures. His thought shows the same characteristic. The truth about man's nature and position in the universe cannot be held steadily, but only momentarily understood, in flashes of perception. The solid, particular, facts of man's physical nature and environment are the raw material in which the spirit moves. And the artist who wishes to represent truth must start from this element, showing it honestly – often stunted and limited. But then at rare moments his gift of imagination will enable him to perceive and to realise the further dimension, the moment of significant vision.

This line of thought, which is consistently developing throughout Carlyle's early writing, leads inevitably to an emphasis on biography and history. The way his mind worked is brought out clearly when he sets out to prove 'how impressive the smallest historical *fact* may become as contrasted with the grandest *fictitious* event'. He records the way in which he was affected by reading in Clarendon's *History of the Rebellion* about King Charles's encounter with a peasant. What attracts Carlyle's attention is the way the single human being emerges from the stream of great events and, though Clarendon's prose, presents himself to another man across such a divide of time: 'We see him but for a moment; for one moment, the blanket of the Night is rent asunder, so that we behold and see, and then closes over him – forever.'[13] What Carlyle chooses to stress is the reality of this incident as the source of its value, and of similar incidents in the biography he is reviewing in the essay: 'Strange power of Reality! Not even this poorest of occurences, but now, after seventy years are come and gone, has a meaning for us. Do but consider that it *true*; that it did in very deed occur!'[14]

In fact, as Carlyle must have reflected, such incidents in history or biography must share an imaginative and consequently a fictional quality, to some degree. But what he was really concerned about was the representation of incidents, characters and experiences, which shared the quality of mundane reality to the fullest degree, and which could yet be shown as significant. They had to be presented visually if they were to be concrete, and so as to excite the mind of the reader to appreciate their significance:

> How are real objects to be *so* seen; on what quality of observing, or of style in describing, does this so intense pictorial power depend? Often a slight circumstance contributes curiously to the result: some little, and perhaps to appearance accidental, feature is presented; a light-gleam, which instantaneously *excites* the mind, and urges it to complete the picture, and evolve the meaning thereof for itself. By critics such light-gleams and their almost magical influence have frequently been noted: but the power to produce such, to select such features as will produce them, is generally treated as a knack, or trick of the trade, a secret for being 'graphic'; whereas these magical feats are in truth, rather inspirations; and the gift of performing them, which acts unconsciously, without forethought, and as if by nature alone, is properly a *genius* for description.[15]

Quite clearly Carlyle is here describing his own method and function as an artist, and also explaining the process by which he came to take an increasing interest in direct historical and social commentary rather than imaginative work.

But, of course, though he went on, in the famous passage from his essay on Diderot, to dismiss the run-of-the-mill novelists, advising them trenchantly, to 'sweep their Novel-fabric into the dust-cart and betake them . . . to understand and record what is *true* . . .',[16] Carlyle never changed his mind about the basic idea. In the Diderot essay he informed his contemporaries: 'Poetry, it will more and more come to be understood, is nothing but Higher Knowledge; and the only genuine Romance . . . Reality'.[17] Years before, writing of Goethe he had declared: 'The end of Poetry is higher: she must dwell in Reality, and become manifest to man in the forms, among which they live and move'.[18] In effect, he argued, throughout his career, art consists in the representation of absolute Reality, embodying the higher truth only on condition that it represents also the actual and concrete circumstances of man. In this respect it had not merely an aesthetic function, but also a moral one, humbling the dreamer and the egoist, reminding men of their fellowship and telling them that truth can be found only in relationships and facts.

No matter how unpalatable Carlyle's later statements on social matters were to his contemporaries, his reputation remains stable well into the later decades of the nineteenth century. And all his contemporaries recognised, as did George Eliot, that his impact had been profound. He did more than any single author, in fact, to settle the foundations of mid-Victorian culture and the Realist movement. He also, indirectly, did a great deal to alter contemporary sensibility in such a way that the novel's great expansion was possible. Though he lacked the imaginative originality and fertility required during the 1830s before new forms and patterns of action could be developed, he did a great deal to bring about circumstances in which they could naturally emerge. It was George Eliot, again, who noticed that in spite of his analytical power, his greatest quality lay 'in concrete presentation'. She praised him for his ability to realise human beings: 'No novelist has made his great ones live for us more thoroughly than Carlyle had made Mirabeau and the men of the French Revolution, Cromwell and the Puritans. What humour in his pictures! Yet what depth of appreciation, what reverence for the great and god-like under every sort of earthly mummery!'[19] John Stuart Mill witnesses to the same effect. He felt Carlyle's influence more directly than Eliot, and knew that it was one of the things which changed his life. He wrote of the *French Revolution* that it bore comparison with Shakespeare, because 'we feel we are in the world of realities: we are among such beings as really could exist, as do exist':

> Never before did we take up a book calling itself by that name, a book treating of past times, and professing to be true, and find ourselves actually among human beings. We at once felt, that what had hitherto been to us mere abstractions had become realities; the 'forms of things unknown' which we fancied we knew, but knew their names merely, were, for the first time, with most startling effect, 'bodied forth' and 'turned into shapes'. Other historians talk to us indeed of human beings; but what do they place before us?[20]

What Mill and Eliot saw was seen by all. Carlyle had shown the English reader much; but above all he had shown that human life, even in its simplest or stupidest forms, could be sublime or terrible, the focal point of forces as powerful as the universe was large. The novelists who followed took what he showed them closely to heart.

Part III

E

9 The Development of Realist Fiction: from Dickens to George Meredith

The years following the accession of Queen Victoria saw a steady increase in the dissemination of Realist ideas until they were apparent in every aspect of English culture. To some extent this may be attributed to the work of Carlyle and Maurice, or to steadily growing awareness of developments in Germany, but all these factors are subordinate parts of the movement by which Romantic ideas came to be assimilated and moulded by contemporary pressures into Victorian Realism. The movement has its own natural logic, which explains other developments in the 1840s when poetry and fiction moved forward into dominance over other literary forms, usurping their functions and themselves undergoing great expansion and development. At a certain stage in their development Realist ideas demanded expression through imaginative literature and especially through the novel, rather than through history, theology, social criticism. The immanence of meaning in experience and the organic unity of life are more naturally displayed in imaginative literature. Yet we must also allow a great deal for the influence of Dickens. His early fiction introduced a new conception of humour, greatly stimulated the development of Victorian sensibility and placed moral considerations firmly in their place above others. Dickens was the first Victorian writer to conceive and attempt the creation of a vision of contemporary life as organically unified, and to face the technical and structural problems which were involved in this. His contemporaries well understood that he held a special place, not only because of his massive popularity, but because he was substantially original – a symptom of wide and deep movements, and an imaginative genius strong enough to mould them. Ironically, Dickens also came to be thought of as an obstacle to the development of Realist ideas. Greater self-awareness, and awareness of purpose, in those contemporaries who had learnt most from his work, made them conscious of him as a force to react against. But in the longer perspective we can see the essential relatedness between Dickens and those who criticised him. Disposition apart, he was working within the same basic framework of ideas and values as Thackeray, George Eliot and George Meredith.

The steady process by which the novel adapted itself to the role it was to play in Victorian culture is partly concealed by the dramatic development of the social novel or novel of purpose in the late 1840s. The Victorian social novel embodies some central Realist ideas. It resulted directly from the work of Carlyle and Maurice and reflected the new 'social morality' which put social and economic ideas under the domain of a sentimental morality. So the emergence of the novel is related to the process by which the Victorian middle classes sought to define themselves and stabilise their context. As John Morley pointed out, this is the main current running through English life in the years preceding the repeal of the Corn Laws in 1846. 'Social sentiment' was the means of stabilising one's view of life as a whole.

We need only look around to recognise the unity of the original impulse which animated men who dreaded or hated one another; and which inspired books that were as far apart as a humouristic novel and a treatise on the sacraments. A great wave of humanity, of benevolence, or desire for

improvement – a great wave of social sentiment, in short –
poured itself among all who had the faculty of large and dis-
interested thinking. The political spirit was abroad in its
most comprehensive sense, the desire of strengthening society
by adapting it to better intellectual ideals. . . .

Notwithstanding their wide diversity of language and of
method, still to all these rival schools and men of genius, the
ultimate end was the same. With all of them the aim to be
attained was social renovation . . .[1]

The Victorian social novel is the direct offshoot of this movement. It is realistic in that it represents the actual state of
society and embodies the idea of integrating social life on a
moral basis. So it represents a step forward in the novel's history, demonstrating its capacity to deal with contemporary
social experience and handle the widest economic and social
questions. But it failed to deal with contemporary experience as
a whole, or to strive towards the structural integrity which was
coming to be the central aim of the Victorian novel.

Charles Kingsley and Mrs Gaskell developed beyond the
point reached in their early social novels, so the essential
superficiality of the social novel as such is better illustrated by
the work of their older contemporary, Benjamin Disraeli. When
he published *Sybil, or the Two Nations* in 1845 Disraeli had
been writing longer than any contemporary of note.[2] Early in
his career he put forward advanced views, arguing that action
should be internalised and that the novel should be used to
investigate the nature of experience and Reality. But he never
appreciated the fact that these new aims required radically new
methods. In his early fiction this was not greatly damaging
because he set out merely to dramatise or display a conception
of life abstractly conceived. Heine praised his *Contarini Fleming*
(1832) not only for its subject – 'the development of a poet' –
but because it combined distinct and contrasting qualities:
'passion and mockery; Gothic richness, the fantasy of the
Saracens and yet overall a classic, even a death-like, repose.'[3]

It is, in fact, one of the rare English novels which shows signs of the process of transition from eighteenth century aims and methods, through Romantic ideas, without actually seizing on the central idea that the value of the imagination's product lies in its wholeness and integrity.

Disraeli's later novels are less abstract. *Coningsby*, in particular, earned praise in England for its sharp satire and penetrating analysis of contemporary politics. In *Sybil* Disraeli tried to make a similar analysis of the social situation, showing the breakdown of communication between classes and the real connectedness that existed below the surface. Certain aspects of the novel are brilliantly executed, showing that Disraeli was well able to learn from Lytton and Dickens. The whole novel, moreover, shows the wit and brilliant fancy which make all his work worth reading still. Yet *Sybil* is seriously defective. As Thackeray pointed out in a review, its plotting and structure are ludicrous:

> A love story (parts of which are charmingly told) is made to connect the two nations together. Sybil, a young person of 'supernatural beauty', is the daughter of a pattern Chartist . . . Of the other nation is Egremont, a dandy aristocrat of not over good blood . . . but being of a kindly disposition, and enamoured of Sybil, he learns to look with more favour on the class to which she belongs, and to see the cruel wrongs under which they labour. They love through three volumes. Sybil (through the medium of Lord John Russell) is rescued from gaol and trial for Chartism; and turning out to be one of the old-old nobility of all, a baroness of forty thousand pounds a year, she marries Egremont; and these two, doubtless, typify the union of the people and the nobles.[4]

The action of *Sybil* is mere machinery, and the novel as a whole a mere vehicle for Disraeli's ideas and social analysis. And in this it is typical of the social novel as a whole, which fails to face up to the aesthetic implications of the moral and philoso-

phic ideas it displays. What George Eliot said of one novel by
Charles Reade has much wider application: 'we feel throughout the presence of remarkable talent, which makes effective
use of materials, but nowhere the genius which absorbs
material, and reproduces it as a living whole.'[5]

The social novel shows the moral and social ideas that result
from an organic conception of life, but not the central idea
itself. Though written with the greatest seriousness, it does
not allow the full importance to the art of representing actual
life. But in the very same years which saw the appearance of
the social novel the deeper view was being consolidated and
was gaining ground. One symptom of this process was the
early phase of the Pre-Raphaelite movement which attacked
mechanical ideas of composition and argued for the choice of
contemporary subjects and the presentation of things as they
are. The process is more consistently and clearly mirrored in
the development of Robert Browning, from the early poetic
drama, *Paracelsus* (1834) to the dramatic monologue. Browning
spent twenty years of his career constantly experimenting with
lyric, narrative and drama, trying to find an aesthetically appropriate medium for his vision of the immanence of spirit in
matter. He found it in the dramatic monologue, which realises
a specific place and time, where a man or woman struggles with
his own apprehension of the spiritual dimension of experience.

The clearest indication of all, however, of the way the tide
was setting towards Realism in mid-Victorian England, is given
by the reception of John Ruskin's *Modern Painters*. The early
volumes of *Modern Painters* (1843 and 1846) did much to con-
solidate Realist ideas and to ground them in aesthetic theory.
Ruskin identified the aesthetic response as essentially moral,
arguing that it consisted in the simultaneous recognition of
structural integrity and moral design. According to Ruskin
man's response to art and to nature was essentially similar,
depending on the sensitivity with which he reconciled sensual
pleasure, sympathetic emotion and spiritual awareness: 'it is

necessary to the existence of an idea of beauty that the sensual pleasure which may be its basis should be accompanied first with joy, then with love of the object, then with a perception of kindness in a superior intelligence, finally with thankfulness and veneration towards the intelligence itself.'[6] Of the various types of beauty which he distinguished, those which most concerned the literary artist involved the honest representation of actuality and the sympathetic emotion through which he came to understand the structural integrity and moral coherence of the object. What Ruskin described as 'Vital Beauty', consisting in the appearance of 'felicitous fulfillment in living things',[7] embodies the Romantic concern for 'the thing in itself' but added a strong emotional and moral dimension. His example, the Alpine flower blooming on the edge of a snowfield, makes a striking impact:

> There is now uttered to us a call for sympathy, now offered to us an image of moral purpose and achievement, which, however unconscious or senseless the creature may be that so seems to call, cannot be heard without affection, nor contemplated without worship, by any of us whose heart is rightly tuned, or whose mind is clearly and surely sighted.[8]

Nearer to the province of the novelist are the modes of art, corresponding to types of beauty, which Ruskin distinguishes as the human ideal and naturalist ideal. The latter, in his terms; 'is that central and highest branch of ideal art which concerns itself simply with things as they ARE . . .'[9] The ideal is achieved through selective arrangement, harmonising individual weaknesses until 'they form a noble whole, in which the imperfection of each several part . . . is absolutely essential, and yet in which whatever is good . . . shall be completely displayed.'[10] The important point in this form of art, Ruskin stresses, is the representation of actual individuals. Similarly, in the human ideal, actual forms are made the basis of a representation which combines strict truth and perfect design:

No face can be ideal which is not a portrait . . . the pursuit
of idealism in humanity, as of idealism in lower nature, can
be successful only when followed through the most constant,
patient and humble rendering of actual models, accompanied
with that earnest mental study of each, which can interpret
all that is written upon it, disentangle the hieroglyphics of
its sacred history, rend the veil of the bodily temple, and
rightly measure the relations of good and evil contending
within it for mastery.[11]

The essence of Ruskin's appeal to his contemporaries lay in
his claim to extend the teaching of Carlyle, demonstrating the
immanence of the ideal in the real, the function of the sympathetic emotions as the connecting link between the world of
the senses and the world of the spirit, and as the medium
through which the integral unity of all aspects of experience
could be embodied. Ruskin provided his contemporaries with
an aesthetic which justified the choice of art, rather than
philosophy or theology, on the highest moral grounds. Outside
the context of the criticism of pictorial and plastic art, moreover, his ideals directed them towards the forms of literature
which could best reproduce the actual and at the same time
demonstrate the importance of the sympathetic emotions as the
means to an understanding of the design of life. Ruskin's
Idealism, in fact, was the Realism of the Victorian novelist.

The connection between Ruskin and Dickens is not to be
studied on the surface, but may be approached through Dickens'
role as a humourist. The importance of his early humorous
fiction is indisputed. *Pickwick Papers* (1836–7), *Oliver Twist*
(1837–8) and *Nicholas Nickleby* (1838–9), were mirrors in which
Victorian readers could study their own sensibility. They made
people conscious of the new forces at work in society and in
themselves, changing them as they read. At the focus of attention of a vast reading public they had an immeasurable effect
on the way people thought and felt. Throughout the formative years when English institutions and manners were chang-

E*

ing under the influence of new ideas, which other writers were presenting in schematic form, Dickens was presenting living pictures of contemporary society, in which these ideas had concrete and particular form. His work was thus the most powerful single force directing those who thought deeply about contemporary life towards the task of representing, rather than analysing, it. His influence, at a deeper level than this, however, was definitive. The development of humour in his hands was closely related to the development of the realist movement. In Dickensian humour pathos and sublimity were brought together with aspects of contemporary experience previously subject to purely comic or farcical treatment, thus preparing the ground for the novelist's serious treatment of all levels and aspects of life. In effect, the concept of humour as it was developing in Victorian theory and being realised in the fictions of the inimitable Boz, could be argued to achieve the aims of all contemporary art.

In Henry Fielding's view, humour was held to arise in the absence of good breeding or good order of the mind. In Sterne's presentation of the Shandy brothers, and in Goldsmith's Vicar of Wakefield, a stronger element of sentiment was introduced, and Scott's Baron Bradwardine marked a further step. In Scott's characters ludicrous manners coexist with intellectual and moral dignity and are attributed to causes in their emotional development and training. After Scott humour continued to change, until it came to be thought, in George Eliot's words, as 'the *sympathetic* presentation of incongruous elements in human nature and life', 'a wonderful and delicious mixture of fun, fancy, philosophy and feeling.'[12] As Carlyle explained, in his essay on Jean Paul Richter, the humourist saw below the incongruities which presented themselves to the critical eye, showing that nobility and sympathy and goodness are unimpaired by grotesque forms of expression and behaviour. According to Carlyle, humour reflects a harmony in the artist's nature, resulting from a deep sympathy which transcends all other motives and reactions:

True humour springs not more from the head than from the heart; it is not contempt, its essence is love; it issues not in laughter, but in still smiles, which live far deeper. It is a sort of inverse sublimity; exalting, as it were, into our affections what is above us. The former is scarcely less precious and heart affecting than the latter; perhaps it is still rarer, and, as a test of genius, still more decisive. It is, in fact, the bloom and perfume, the purest effluence of a deep, fine loving nature, a nature in harmony with itself, reconciled to the world and its stintedness and contradiction, nay finding in this very contradiction new elements of beauty as well as goodness.[18]

Carlyle himself was slow to recognise the essential seriousness of Dickens' early fictions, but they were widely recognised as embodying the conception of humour he had outlined. Characters like Bumble, Pecksniff, Sam Weller and Mrs Gamp, combine within themselves apparently irreconcilable vitality and stuntedness, attracting sympathy which completely transcends the moral scheme of the novels in which they are found. And in the view of the narrator himself – benevolent and critical, passionate and satirical – contemporaries detected precisely that 'deep, fine loving nature' which helped them to find new elements of beauty and goodness in the world around them. In spite of the inconsistency and incoherence of his early work, Dickens' humour lifted it beyond criticism and drew the strongest praise even from those most practised in the application of eighteenth century ideas of probability and order.

Dickens' achievement, of course, went still further, even though there were some of his readers for whom the humour of the early books represented a height which could not be surpassed. In each successive novel he expressed more clearly and coherently a view of life of which humorous characterisation was but one aspect. In the novels preceding *Dombey and Son* (1846), and in the early Christmas stories, he worked out a coherent criticism of social relations and a system of moral values based on the idea of man's predominant need for affection and relatedness. As this view became clearer be gained greater control as a novelist, and the clumsy stitching of *Nicholas Nickleby* and *Martin Chuzzlewit* was replaced by his later method in which thematic values received materially appropriate form. In *Dombey and Son* he abandoned much of the scaffolding that had held earlier novels together. Though his narrator there retains control of selection, sequence and proportion, his control is largely justified by the way in which thematic values relate to dramatic values, so that the whole action seems a natural unit of experience. If maturity is marked by complete control, then Dickens' mature work actually begins with *David Copperfield* (1849–50), but even so, it is not too much to say that *Dombey and Son* is the first English novel in which an organic view of life is given organic form.

Ironically the point at which Dickens achieved complete control over his own art was also the point at which he first came under serious and sustained attack. No doubt this can partly be attributed to the way in which his career developed. *David Copperfield* stands out from his other novels in several ways. It is the most autobiographical, suggesting that its composition involved a process of self-examination. Running side by side for several months with Thackeray's *Pendennis*, which has strong points of similarity, it marks as well as anything can the moment when the Victorian novel achieved its full status. Yet it is also strangely untypical in some respects. *David Copperfield* is Dickens' most optimistic novel, and the one in which his idiosyncracies of manner and attitude are least clearly marked. His later development was along harsher and more sombre lines, which left some admirers dissatisfied. The increasing element of fantasy and satire unsettled even John Forster: and David Masson, an intelligent and by no means unsympathetic critic, echoed the views of many when he attacked the tendencies to 'extravagance and caricature' which seemed to be becoming more pronounced with the appearance of every later novel.

Dickens' outspoken and sometimes ill-considered social

criticism and satire also earned him some animosity, and it was
to this that John Forster attributed the hostile criticisms of the
years after the mid-century. A later, and perhaps similarly partial
critic has described how, at this time, 'the seeds of revolution
were being sown by gifted and perceptive readers who had out-
grown his books'.

> It was to be a revolution initiated by a critical aristocracy,
> through whose efforts Thackeray, and later Eliot and Mere-
> dith, were to be thrust forward as leading contendors for the
> emminence occupied by Dickens. The manifestoes for such a
> revolution were published during this period. They include
> the reviews in which Fitzjames Stephen demonstrated that a
> romantic's criticism of society was both repulsive and fatuous,
> and they include the essays in which G. H. Lewes demon-
> strated that a romantic's handling of probability was naïvely
> out of keeping with the requirements of realism and of mature
> taste.[14]

In fact, rather than a revolution produced by a fastidious
aristocracy what happened was the natural and inevitable
development of the culture to which Dickens was making a
massive but idiosyncratic contribution. Increasingly, after the
mid-1840s, a movement of conscious realism developed. It drew
strength from the example of Goethe and an acquaintance with
developments throughout Europe, especially the novels of
George Sand, Balzac and Flaubert, but was fundamentally an
English movement. It was a movement by writers whom one
could almost describe as brought to life by Dickens, firmly fixed
in the world he had brought to light, who were yet finding
themselves at odds with him in certain essential respects vital
to the development of art and life as they saw it.

The new critical note resulted from a feeling among educated
readers that Dickens was avoiding the most problematic areas
of modern experience and offending against the most important
criteria of taste and judgement. Dickens seemed to ignore the
moral and philosophical issues that arose from contemporary

concern with the relationship between freedom and dignity and the determinist pressures at work on the individual. His contemporaries agreed with him about the positive values in human character and human society and accepted his view of their connectedness. But they were unable to accept his absolute assertion of values, which seemed to conflict with modern awareness of the actual processes by which societies and states of mind came into being. For a minority of Dickens' readers – rightly termed a 'critical aristocracy' – the main business of fiction was the representation of processes of causality, comprising internal pressures and external influences. Probability and analysis, the representation of the working of material laws, were superimposed on the artist's fundamental purpose of demonstrating the unity and meaningfulness of experience. So in the English fiction of the period 1850 to 1880 the dominant task facing the novelist became the representation and reconciliation of physical law and spiritual truth. Contemporaries often expressed it as the reconciliation of Realism and Idealism. In effect it amounted to the attempt to embody romantic values according to the terms of science. Realism was the mode, Idealism the original impetus and the ultimate aim.

The distinction between Idealism and Realism provided contemporaries with a useful method of describing what they felt to be the essential difference between Dickens and Thackeray. David Masson was by no means alone in thinking of Dickens as a novelist of the 'Ideal, or Romantic School', creator of a world of semi-fantastic conditions where the laws need not be 'those of ordinary probability', as distinct from Thackeray, an artist of the Real School, whose aim was 'to represent life as it is actually and historically.'[15] The central difference lay in the representation of character. The adherents of either novelist praised or blamed them according to the extent to which they thought of the analysis of motivation as leading to the discovery of truth or as undermining confidence in the essential goodness of human nature. In his biography of Dickens, Forster constantly defended his friend by means of implicit criticisms of Thackeray's method. The characters in Dickens' novels, Forster thought, combined an 'impression of reality' with elements of universal human truth. His failure to analyse them related to the fact that his vision was essentially objective rather than subjective and the result of his method was the presentation of the way in which human beings relate one to another:

> To expound or discuss his creations, to lay them psychologically bare, to analyse their organisms, to subject to minute demonstration their fibrous and other tissues, was not at all Dickens' way. His genius was his fellow feeling with his race; his mere personality was never the bound or limit to his perceptions, however strongly sometimes it might colour them; he never stopped to dissect or anatomise his own work; but no man could better adjust the outward and visible oddities in a delineation to its inner and unchangeable veracities.[16]

Forster's objection to analysis lay deeper, though, than is suggested here. He shared with Dickens a fundamental distaste for the whole business of analysis on the grounds that it tended to conceal the essential goodness of human nature and to debase it. Rather pointedly Forster commented that it was better to 'paint men pleasantly, than to describe society as a gay fair in which every man puts forward what is best in him, and hides his raggedness.' Too close a concentration on the complexities of motivation, Forster thought, distracted attention from the understanding of human nature itself. Every man, sharing the stuff of which all are made, must possess a source of virtue which is untainted even when his character is debased:

> The heart of every man who is no better or no worse than the mass of his neighbours, will tell him distinctly that the words knows nothing of, because he himself shrinks from telling to the world, the holiest and best part of his nature. Secret aspirations, untold sacrifices, hidden charities, thoughts of the warmest good-will and friendship between man and

man which very rarely rise into expressions of equivalent intensity – these things lie under the calm surface of a thousand faces; and such secrets are kept more wisely, and lie a thousand times more frequently unseen, than any vice or folly that we try to hide. Every man knows that his lips would stammer, and his cheeks burn, if he attempted to abondon the reserve which keeps the brightest spark of the divine nature – not extinguished in the basest of us – deep in his heart, away from the eyes of many, and safe from daily comment.[17]

On this point Forster and Dickens would have agreed. So would John Ruskin, whose appreciation of Dickens was no more than partial, but who shared his revulsion from Thackerayan analysis. Ruskin thought that Thackeray 'settled like a meat fly on whatever one had for dinner and made one sick of it'. According to him, the tendency of Thackeray's work was blasphemous – he was guilty of ' "Harmful speaking" – not against God only, but against man, and against all the good works and right purposes of Nature.' The juxtaposition in *Vanity Fair* of the picture of Amelia praying for her husband's safety with the reference to George lying dead at Waterloo seemed to him a cynical denial of the efficacy of prayer and the meaningfulness of spiritual experience – 'blasphemy of the most fatal and subtle kind.'[18]

Many Victorian critics of the 1850s and 1860s shared something of this discomfort in the presence of Thackeray's incisive analysis of contemporary modes of thought and feeling, but more echoed Masson's opinion that Thackeray combined strength of understanding, acquired knowledge and exquisiteness of literary taste to a hitherto unprecedented degree. George Eliot spoke of him 'as I suppose the majority of people with any intellect do', as 'on the whole the most powerful of living novelists'.[19] George Meredith thought him 'the most perfect Artist in prose that I know of'.[20] To Charlotte Brontë he was 'a Titan of mind', 'the first of modern masters'; and on more than one occasion she gave it as her opinion that 'if Truth were again a goddess, Thackeray would be her high priest.'[21]

There is no doubt that contemporaries, even if they disliked his work, thought of Thackeray, compared to Dickens, as an intellectual, and even if modern readers will be less willing to think of his intellect as more incisive or penetrating than that of the creator of *Bleak House* or *Great Expectations*, it cannot be denied even now that he had grasped intellectually the nature of contemporary moral and intellectual problems and reflected deeply on their representation in art. The basis of Thackeray's attitude to life was humanistic – in common with Eliot and Meredith, he rejected formulas and orthodoxies which claimed to contain spiritual truth and looked rather to the natural world as an end in itself. Though Ruskin might not have recognised it, their views were basically similar, because Thackeray also associated the sympathetic emotions with spiritual and aesthetic awareness. Like Ruskin, too, he kept his gaze firmly fixed on the world, around him, though, characteristically, he refused to read it as a Divine Book. Art, he thought, should consist in the honest and diligent study of that world. He wrote to Mrs Brookfield:

> I don't know about the Unseen World, the use of the Seen World is the right thing, I'm sure – it is just as much God's work and creation as the kingdom of heaven with all the angels . . . the bounties of the Father I believe to be count-less and inexhaustible for most of us here in life – Love the greatest [,] Art (which is an exquisite and admiring sense of Nature [,] the next. By Jove, I'll admire if I can, the wing of a cocksparrow as much as the pinion of an archangel and admire God the Father of the Earth, earthy, first, waiting for the completion of my senses and the fulfillment of his intentions towards [me] afterwards when this scene closes over us.[22]

In all probability Dickens would have agreed with this state-ment, but it was actually the basis for Thackeray of a rejection of Dickens's art as an exaggerated and distorted representation of nature. Thackeray appreciated to the full Dickens' presentation of benevolence and love at work in human nature: 'Thankfully I take my share of the feast of love and kindness which this gentle, and generous, and charitable soul has contributed to the happiness of the world.'[23] In his own role as humourist he tried not to forget that 'if Fun is good, Truth is still better, and Love best of all'.[24] Yet he seems to have thought it an essential part of his own function as novelist – as 'weekday preacher' – to combine sympathy with absolute truthfulness and to present a humane examination of human character with the tools and the methods of pathological analysis.

Thackeray was fully aware of the charges made against him in the Dickens camp. He responded briskly to Robert Bell's description of *Vanity Fair* as 'so full of petty vices and grovelling passions.'[25]

> If I had put in more fresh air, as you call it, my object would have been defeated – It is to indicate, in cheerful terms, that we are for the most part an abominably foolish and selfish people 'desperately wicked' and all eager after vanities.[26]

Later in the same letter he refers to Forster's remarks that he is inferior to Fielding (and by inference to Dickens) in his lack of 'large cordiality' which might have raised him into the region of 'simple uncontaminated human affection . . .'[27]

> You have all of you taken my misanthropy to task – I wish I could myself; but take the world by a certain standard (you know what I mean) and who dares talk of having any virtue at all? For instance Forster says after a scene with Blifil, the air is cleared by a laugh of Tom Jones – Why Tom Jones in my holding is as big a rogue as Blifil. Before God he is – I mean the man is selfish according to his nature as Blifil according to his.[28]

Another passage in this letter gives us a clue to the extent to which Thackeray thought of the debate in which he was

engaged as central to Victorian culture as a whole. An important part of the thinking behind *Vanity Fair* was provoked by
Carlyle's statements about fiction in his *Miscellaneous Criticism.*
It was from that source that Thackeray derived the idea of 'the
long-eared narrator' who is seen addressing the crowd from the
up-turned barrel on the cover of the novel's monthly parts. It
was probably the same essay which gave him the title of the
novel and the idea which transformed it from 'Pen and Pencil
Sketches of English Society' into a full-scale analysis of contemporary life. He was content to play the role of the long-eared
tale-teller, addressing fools, because his whole view of life
derived from an awareness of his own state of consciousness.
The figure of speech with which he illustrates this point gives
interesting evidence about the processes of thought which preceded his sudden emergence to major status with *Vanity
Fair:*

> . . . I want to leave everybody dissatisfied and unhappy at the
> end of the story – we ought all to be with our own and all
> other stories. Good God, don't I see *(in that may-be cracked
> and warped looking glass in which I am always looking)* my
> own weaknesses, wickednesses, lusts, follies, shortcomings? in
> company let us hope with better qualities about which we
> will pretermit discourse. We must lift up our voices about
> these and howl to a congregation of fools: so much at least
> has been my endeavour.[29]

This image of the novelist examining the cracked mirror of his
own consciousness is brought to mind again by the title page to
the volume edition of the novel, probably designed some time
after the completion of the number publication in July 1848.
It seems to have been suggested by a phrase used by his friend
John Sterling in a famous review of Carlyle's *Miscellaneous
Criticism.* Carlyle's essays, together with Sterling's commentary,
comprise, in the widest terms, a debate on the essential question
which divided Dickens and Thackeray.

In the first place, though an admiring and thoroughly appre-

ciative review of Carlyle's work, Sterling's article criticised his
friend's obscurantism regarding science and scientific analysis.
His own attitude was that the developments of the modern
intellect represented healthy progress rather than disease and
provided contemporary man with criteria of judgement to
replace those offered by authority, by the senses, or by unaided
intuition:

> It is an all but immeasurable change, that science has now
> and for ever seized the right of deciding on the premisses
> which she shall admit, – is not merely bound to the duty of
> accepting those supplied to her, whether by the decrees of
> church councils and theologians, or by the creeds and canons
> of the bodily senses.[30]

Accepting this change led Sterling towards a kind of humanism
basically similar to that of Thackeray and his successors, Meredith and Eliot. It was an attitude closely connected with the
dominance of the realist novel as a method of interpreting contemporary life.

> Leaving to religion its own practical rights, which are ever-
> lasting, and which no other power can arrogate, science now
> postulates only what is essential to the scientific construction
> of knowledge. She leaves the feelings of reverence and duty
> to glorify, as conscience, and faith require, the principle
> which she herself acknowledges as the highest affirmation of
> the intelligence and the essence of all being; but she refuses
> to accept their representation of her primal truth as that
> which is valid for her. This crisis, which has expelled from
> the sanctuary of pure intuition everything but that ideal
> which is necessary as a centre for consistent thought, and
> has left external tradition and assertion, however, authorised,
> to fill only their appropriate place in the affections of prac-
> tical life, has made philosophy a new and independent world,
> surrounding with its diaphanous circle the sphere of all other
> knowledge and belief.[31]

The logic of Sterling's conclusion is marred slightly by the fact that in Victorian society it was not to philosophy that the new and independent world belonged, but to fiction, but his basic point is actually strengthened by the later movement to unify fiction and philosophy. His argument proceeded to take into account an aspect of Carlyle's statement which is more particularly relevant to the business of the novelist. Carlyle had identified self-consciousness as the modern disease, leading to disorientation and loss of purpose. Sterling was well aware from his own experience of the price one paid in doubt and self-torment for the benefits of self-awareness and the rational, analytic intellect, but he still saw it as a necessary characteristic of modern life and even as a means of reaching the higher degree of Truth to which modern man seemed in process of attaining.

Sterling saw the individual as an organism built according to the same laws as society, the animate and even the inanimate world. Consequently he understood that self-examination was a necessary prelude to the understanding of life as a whole:

> Self-intuition and self-interpretation, when the self is re-garded as a product of higher forces, similar to the other, and especially to the human, products of the same, is indispensible to all the true knowledge of man and men, and even of all other things, in that chief sense in which their essence is a reality analagous to us. The exploring of myself in this higher view is not a nourishing, but a correcting, of vanity. Self is thus resolved into a result, an exponent, of laws, which it depends on, not commands – is valued for the sake of that which is above it, – is disindividualised, unisolated, rather universalized and idealized.[32]

Sterling must have intended this passage primarily as a defence of the Romantic poets against early Victorian suspicion, but it has much wider reference. His argument is a defence of modern sensibility against the attacks of all those who identified subjectivity and sickness and those who closed any area of modern consciousness from the researches of the novelist. Sterling's attitude clearly belongs within the tradition of Victorian humanism, where rationalism could be accepted and put to work in the service of art, and where the methods of scientific study of man's nature were most confidently employed. It helps to see Thackeray, too, within this tradition, when we notice that he had read this essay closely and had taken one part of it to himself. Sterling distinguished between large-minded study of one's own nature as typical of nature in general and narrow concern with one's own personality: 'My consciousness', he says, 'is the window, the only possible one, through which I look at the universe.' But: 'My individuality is the looking glass, always a small, often a cracked and dim one, that hangs on the inner wall of the same chamber.'[33] He advocates looking through the window of the soul because it brightens and enlarges itself in the process, while gazing in the mirror 'is the proceeding of coxcombs and quacks.' It was as coxcomb and quack that Thackeray presented himself in *Vanity Fair*, written in a consciously minor key, and attempting not to expand and universalise, but to present in all its dreariness and triviality, the texture of contemporary moral and social life.

Sterling and Carlyle disagreed sharply about attitudes and methods, but were in agreement about basic values. So were Dickens and Thackeray. And even the later, self-conscious, exponents of a more critical and scientific realism than Thackeray's preserved this fundamental agreement. We can see this in the criticism of G. H. Lewes, who is important not only because of his relationship with George Eliot, but also because he was among the most intelligent and self-aware of Victorian critics and one of the first to develop a theory of Realism. Lewes's thought is an extension of Ruskin's. His central idea is that Life and Art must be seen as complete and meaningful in themselves, but this can only be done when the individual learns to achieve unity and harmony within himself. The sceptic-hero of his best (unfinished) novel, is converted to this view by a humanist-friend:

'. . . Look here! man's nature is three-fold: it is passionate emotional and rational. Each of these modes of activity is fundamental, and has its own laws. Passion has its instincts; Emotion has its *sentiment:* Reason has its *logic* . . .

'Now as each of these portions of our being has its own laws, none of them are amenable to the others . . .'

'Is religion then a question of emotion?'

'Eminently.'

'Then how can you expect men to believe?'

'I expect them to *feel*.'

'Is feeling to be taken as a proof?'

'The best of proofs! What, for instance, do you *know* (logically) of Life? Can you form an idea – a distinct idea – of Life? You cannot. What do you *know* of Love? Nothing; yet is there no such thing as Life, is there no such truth as Love? . . . If you can believe in Life and Love . . . If you have within you a faculty for their appreciation, – have you not also a faculty for the appreciation of the universal Life, the the universal Love?'

'You must be right!' exclaimed Armand. 'And that is why, in spite of my reason, my *feeling* has always struggled against my arguments.'[34]

The capacity for emotion, and particularly for love, is the faculty which permits the individual to reach this understanding but only when it is extended and purified by moral feeling.

A similar view of human psychology underlies Lewes's criticism of fiction, and especially his idea of Realism, which was the product of a long period of study and reading. Early in his career as a critic he abandoned mechanistic ideas and argued that the work of art should be independent of intrusive moral criteria. At this stage, however, he mistrusted, at any rate superficial Realism, and praised George Sand above Balzac because of the lyrical or 'poetic' element in her novels. Later he stressed the expressive quality of art against its imitative character, but at the same time developed great respect for the

art of Jane Austen, whose solid realistic qualities he compared
with Shakespeare's. And gradually he brought these two aspects
of his thought together in a theory of Realism closely similar to
George Eliot's and George Meredith's, which like theirs, owed
a great deal to Ruskin's description of Idealism. Lewes depended
on the sympathetic imagination of the artist (related to the sympathetic emotion of the reader or observer) as a means of reconciling his view of art as expressive of the artist's imaginative
vision, with his appreciation for Realistic observation:

> We may now come to an understanding on the significance
> of the phrase Idealism in Art. Suppose two men equally gifted
> with the perceptive powers and technical skill necessary to
> the accurate representation of a village group, but the one
> to be gifted, over and above these qualities, with an emotional
> sensibility which leads him to sympathise intensely with the
> emotions playing amid the village group. Both will delight in
> the forms of external nature, both will lovingly depict the
> scene and scenery; but the second will not be satisfied there-
> with: his sympathy will lead him to express something of
> the emotional life of the group; the mother in his picture will
> not only hold her child in a graceful attitude, she will look
> at it with a mother's tenderness . . . Without once departing
> from strict reality, he will have thrown a sentiment into his
> group which every spectator will recognise as poetry.[35]

Is not this artist, Lewes asks, 'more *real*' than one who confines
himself to externals? The fundamental assumption is that life,
as well as art, becomes meaningful by virtue of the emotions,
refined to moral feelings. Only art which embodies this truth
can be referred to as Realist, which is another term for Truth
itself:

> Art is a Representation of Reality . . . limited by the nature
> of its medium: . . . but while thus limited . . . Art always
> aims at the representation of Reality, i.e. of Truth; and no
> departure from truth is permissible . . . Realism is thus the
> basis of all Art, its antithesis is not Idealism, but *Falsism*.[36]

Lewes's ideas are easily recognised in the early fiction and criticism of George Eliot, but it is not sufficient to explain their influence on her in personal terms. The mutual influence of these two writers resulted from a deep common agreement over basic attitudes and values, which can be traced throughout mid-Victorian literature, even in the work of men with whom in some respects they most bitterly disagreed. One of the most fundamental elements in mid-Victorian thought was the sense of opposition between intellect and emotion. Victorian artists and intellectuals were preoccupied with this factor because they were sentimentalists, convinced that value and meaning were attainable only through the emotions. But below this, at the very deepest level, they all experienced the need to reconcile the opposing elements. Dickens took one way of doing this, similar to that taken by Carlyle and Ruskin. Thackeray, less optimistic, and more conscious of the relativity of values, took another, which was in some ways self-consciously designed as a corrective to Dickens. The attitudes dictated in their cases by temperament and upbringing, however, became symptomatic, for other Victorians, of the latent opposition in life itself. There is little doubt that the immediate and widespread popularity of George Eliot's fiction arose from the fact that it was felt to go a good way towards reconciling these attitudes — and so of fulfilling the most essential function of all Realist art.

George Eliot seemed to many contemporaries to stand on firmer ground than her predecessors — and, indeed, it might well he said that she did. Throughout the nineteenth century, as she was well aware, rationalism has made steady advance, and yet at the same time, up to the seventh decade, it had been progressively affected by Romantic attitudes, especially organicism. It was beginning to appear after the middle of the century that the new sciences, geology, biology, anthropology and etymology, were the result of a tendency to study the nature of things in themselves rather than continuations of eighteenth century habits of analysis. Even Biblical criticism, which had once seemed to threaten all belief in a non-material dimension, worked in the same direction, throwing new light on Jesus as the Type of all men. Most of all, the development of evolutionary ideas helped in the extension and consolidation of realism. For evolution gave a new and firmer basis for the reconciliation of moral, social and intellectual values. On this basis George Eliot and George Meredith built, assimilating the most advanced ideas and pushing the novel forward step by step with the development of the modern consciousness. Their success in this respect tends to obscure the fact that even in their latest work – in Meredith's case as late as 1896 – they were working from premises formed long before: the fundamental premises of mid-Victorian Realism.

10 The Realism of Dickens

Of all the great Victorian writers Dickens was the first to receive critical rehabilitation in the twentieth century, after the last certainties of Victorianism had crumbled away. From the modern standpoint, Dickens seems to have escaped from the limitations of Victorian Realism and penetrated to a deeper level of reality. The modern reader tends to see him through the eyes of Dostoevsky and Kafka. The developments of bureaucracy and totalitarianism have justified the radical and imaginative criticism of Victorian society which contemporaries found grotesquely exaggerated. The fundamental social optimism of his contemporaries compares poorly with the harsher vision of his later novels, where the institutions of society became ominous and menacing, threatening the inner life of the individual and of humanity itself. His concern with abnormal states of mind and his penetrating view of the more obscure forces at work in human character give his work a powerful appeal to generations taught by the experience of total war and genocide to look for the principles of character in areas beyond the reach of consciousness. So now, what critics like G. H. Lewes were tempted to explain by referring to Dickens' lack of education, or his mental unbalance, we select as indicating his possession of creative imagination beyond the reach of the contemporaries whose reputation once seemed more firmly based than his own. Yet we need to bear in mind what Dickens' continuing popularity with the mass of the Victorian reading public indicates. He was original and idiosyncratic, but he was also typical. His work embodies principles and impulses central to Victorian culture; and the framework of his imagination was built up only with the materials available within it. If he transcends some of the limitations of Victorian Realism, it is nevertheless on that firm ground that he stands.

Allowing for the change of mood which contemporaries noticed after *David Copperfield*, we can see that the elements of Dickens' later view of life were identical with those which underlay the lively humour and pathos of *Pickwick* and the drama of David's story. Dickens' view of life was essentially dynamic. He saw mankind inhabiting a world of harsh material conditions, informed by forces beyond his power or direct comprehension. Man himself, in Dickens' view, is a focus of those forces, a creature of energies which are beyond the control of the conscious mind. He is physically weak and vulnerable, likely to be stunted by circumstances or destroyed by his own passions. Over this view Dickens imposed a moral framework which emphasises the importance of sentiment and affection and suggests that the will can be educated to allow the individual to control his character and destiny and achieve happiness. Domestic relations, social groups, and at times, society as a whole, seemed to him to offer contexts in which this aim could be realised. Yet the essential combination of weakness and power remained unaltered, and as his career developed he came to see more clearly the vulnerability of the individual and the way in which mankind as a whole, acting through social institutions, could create an environment in which certain forms of life were made possible only at the cost of terrifyingly destructive conditions.

This view of human nature governed Dickens' whole approach to characterisation. It determined his absorption with abnormal psychological states, with acts of crime and the individual's relation to them, and underlay the vivid presentation of characters like Mr Bumble, Mr Pecksniff, Quilip and Mrs Gamp. Their appeal overrides their function in the moral scheme of the novels which they inhabit. Each of them acts out an unending drama for the benefit of the reader and for themselves. They are the centre of energies and impulses they cannot control, the victims of a triumphant vitality which is constantly frustrated but constantly expresses itself through tormented speech, inconsistent action and grotesque mannerism.

The same factor sometimes affects Dickens' characterisation adversely. In representing psychological processes, he is hampered by his awareness of the forces moving within individuals, and through relationships. Through this he was committed to a melodramatic and sensational treatment of character, presenting internal processes by external factors. So one of the most important moments in *Dombey and Son,* which reflects brilliant psychological penetration, is marred by awkwardness. When Dombey reproaches and attempts to domineer over Edith, it is a moment of crisis in their relationship and in her whole life. Through blind egoism and insensitivity he chooses the worst possible moment to assert himself. Edith is held back from outright defiance only by her love for Florence; and his behaviour is a powerful new element urging her to violent reaction:

'I think', she answered, 'that I understand you very well.' She looked upon him as she said so, and folding her white arms sparkling with gold and gems, upon her swelling breast, turned away her eyes.

If she had been less handsome, and less stately in her cold composure, she might not have had the power of impressing him with the sense of disadvantage that penetrated through his utmost pride... The very diamonds – a marriage gift – that rose and fell impatiently upon her bosom, seemed to pant to break the chain that clasped them round her neck, and roll down on the floor where she might tread upon them . . .

She bent her eyes upon him steadily, and set her trembling lips. He saw her bosom throb, and saw her face flush and turn white. All this he could know and did: but he could not know that one word was whispered in the deep recesses of her heart, to keep her quiet; and that word was Florence.

Blind idiot, rushing to a precipice! He thought she stood
in awe of *him!*

'You are too expensive madam', said Mr. Dombey . . . 'I
beg that Mrs. Granger's very different experiences may now
come to the instruction of Mrs. Dombey.'

Still the fixed look, the trembling lips, the throbbing
breast, the face now crimson and now white; and the deep
whisper Florence, Florence, speaking to her in the beating
of her heart.[1]

It is a necessary part of this scene that Dombey should only
observe Edith from the outside, with no understanding of her
character, but it is significant that Dickens makes us share his
point of view for the most part and derives most of the tension
of the episode from the difference in the state of mind of the
protagonists. Dickens sees the psychological stress which Edith
endures as the result of forces working within her, not identifiable as parts of her consciousness, but greater than that,
threatening to overwhelm her and sweep her along on a course
of action for which she is only partly prepared. At this point
they are held back by great self-control, the joint product of
pride and love, which preoccupies her consciousness and dictates her behaviour. But this is not the whole story by any
means. Indeed, an important part of Edith's problem arises
from her own awareness of her body as an object, leading to
moments of intense self-disgust and often to self-inflicted blows.
To enter Edith's consciousness would actually prevent Dickens
from suggesting much of this, and prevent him, too, from
expressing the absolute sense of non-communication which the
physical confrontation conveys. So he concentrates on externals.
He puts before us the statuesque calmness which is what Dombey
sees, and the signs of physical disturbance which he misinter-
prets – the bosom's rise and fall, and its throbbing; her flush
and pallor: and then he introduces, as a constant point of
reference, what Dombey cannot hear – the voice rather melodramatically whispering, 'in the deep recesses of her heart'. The

result of the whole passage is a sense of mingled strength and weakness, which recurs in the later novels whenever Dickens tries to bring into the open the forces which move character beyond the reach of reason, and especially in scenes of confrontation which produce violent psychological reactions.

It was a long time before Dickens obtained full control or even full awareness of the deeper elements in his imaginative vision which controlled the development of his art. In his early fiction there is often a degree of tension between these elements and the moral view derived from them. In 'Ginshops', for example, the social and moral purpose of the narrator is constantly broken through by his awareness of the vitality and humour of the scene he is describing:

> The filthy and miserable appearance of this part of London can hardly be imagined by those (and there are many such) who have not witnessed it. Wretched houses with broken windows patched with rags and paper; every room let out to a different family, and in many instances to two or even three – fruit and 'sweet-stuff' manufacturers in the cellars, barbers and red-herring vendors in the first floor, three families on the second, starvation in the attics, Irishmen in the passage, a 'Musician' in the front kitchen, and a charwoman and five hungry children in the back one – filth everywhere – a gutter before the houses, and a drain behind – clothes drying and slops emptying from the windows; girls of fourteen or fifteen with matted hair, walking about barefoot, and in white greatcoats, almost their only covering; boys of all ages, in coats of all sizes and no coats at all; men and women, in every variety of scanty and dirty apparel, lounging, scolding, drinking, smoking, squabbling, fighting and swearing.[2]

The moral tone set in the opening lines and picked up again in the reference to the destitute condition of the adolescent girls, is not consistently held. The constantly changing pitch, the parcelling out of the house among incongruous groups and occupations, the switching from one type of generalisation to another – from starvation to Irishmen – the glimpse of washing and slops drying and emptying themselves with apparent independence, and finally the effective building up of verbs of violent action, leave the reader with an overwhelming sense of vitality which overrides the suggestion that the human beings living in the conditions so described are stunted and limited.

In *Oliver Twist* the fascination with the vital principle at work, again in a morally ambiguous form, appears in the treatment of Bill Sykes' pursuit by the mob of citizens. Sykes' murder of Nancy outrages the ideas which are central to the book's moral scheme, arousing a painful sense of pathos and sympathy for the victim, which is stronger by virtue of the fact that she has begun to be capable of moral responsiveness. It is the result of a mechanical response at the lowest possible level of feeling, in a nature brutalised to the point that it is insensitive of the connection between moral and emotional life. The murderer is pursued after the deed, not by his conscience, but by his imagination, a faculty more difficult to silence. By his imagination he is drawn back to London and his old haunts and associates and into the midst of the huge and violent crowd which yells for his blood. Sykes is driven to bay by an excited mob which is passionately absorbed in his capture :

There was another roar. At this moment the word was passed among the crowd that the door was forced at last and that he who had first called for the ladder had mounted into the room. The stream abruptly turned as this intelligence ran from mouth to mouth, and the people at the windows, seeing those upon the bridges pouring back, quitted their stations, and running into the street, joined the concourse that now thronged pell mell to the spot they had left; each man crushing and striving with his neighbour, and all panting with impatience to get near the door, and look upon the criminal as the officers brought him out. The cries and shrieks of those who were pressed almost to suffocation or trampled down and trodden under foot in the confusion, were dreadful; the narrow ways were completely blocked up; and at this time, between the rush of some to regain the space in front of the house, and the unavailing struggles of others to extricate themselves from the mass, the immediate attention was distracted from the murderer, although the universal eagerness for his capture was, if possible, increased.[3]

Their original motivating impulse was the laudable disapproval of Sykes' murderous brutality, but by this time the crowd is acting with a similar passion, murderous towards the murderer and callously destructive towards each other. The hunter and the hunted remain distinct according to the novel's moral scheme, but a strong element of ambiguity is introduced which partially obscures it, bringing out instead Dickens' underlying perception of the essentially passionate nature of all men. The ambiguity is resolved when Sykes hangs himself. Superficially at odds with the crowd, he is at a deeper level at one with them – it is his imagination, fixated by the memory of his action, that makes him identify the eyes of the dog with those of the murdered girl, causing him to start, lose his balance and fall to the end of the rope. So we see that as an imaginative vision, the novel is coherent, though its superficial scheme of benevolent sentiment pales before the harsher, more violent image of man's nature which inspires it.

Later in Dickens' work his interest in the forces at work in human character and in life as a whole begins to play a greater part in determining the shape of his novels. *Dombey and Son* is apparently centred on the moral development of Dombey during the period between the death of his wife and his final acceptance of his need for his daughter. But there are times in the novel when the focus is entirely removed from Dombey and even from the surrounding characters who support the novel's moral scheme, and at these times we become aware of factors at work which are only dimly reflected in the central story. These passages hold together in the imagination of the reader, suggesting that there are forces at work in Dickens' imagination of which, at this stage, he is only partially aware. One of them occurs when Dickens is describing Dombey's state of mind during the journey to Birmingham with Major Bagstock. The passage is given from Dombey's point of view, but registers what he does not see – that is, the variety and vitality of human character and situation. To the reader the countless and breathless succession of objects and impressions associated with the train's headlong, impetuous movement, gives an overwhelming impression of the force of life which the train itself symbolises. To Dombey, who is isolated from Florence and from the world by pride, the train seems rather to suggest the remorseless power of death. Yet although Dombey is wilfully wrong in his attitude to life, his view is given as much authority as its apparent opposite, so that the final result of the passage is to imply the proximity of connectedness of both life and death:

> Away, with a shriek, and a roar, and a rattle, from the town, burrowing among the dwellings of man and making the streets hum, flashing out into the meadows for a moment, mining in through the damp earth, booming on in darkness and heavy air, bursting out again into the sunny day so bright and wide; away, with a shriek and a roar and a rattle, through the fields, through the woods, through the corn, through the hay, through the chalk, through the mould, through the clay, through the rock, among objects close at hand, almost in the grasp, ever flying from the traveller, and a deceitful distance ever moving slowly within him: like as in the track of the remorseless monster, Death!
>   . . . away with a shriek and a roar and a rattle, and no trace to leave behind but dust and vapour: like as in the track of the remorseless monster, Death!
>   . . . Away, and still away . . . glimpses of cottage homes, of old roads, and paths that look deserted, small and insignificant as they are left behind; and so they are, and what else is

there, but such glimpses in the track of the indomitable monster, Death![4]

Significantly, it is the train which kills Carker, by no means merely as the result of coincidence, but by some kind of natural logic, of which the doomed man is himself aware. After his initial escape from Dombey he becomes conscious of an irrational and obscure terror of a force outside himself:

> Some other terror came upon him, and quite removed from this of being pursued, suddenly like an electric shock, as he was creeping through the streets. Some visionary terror, unintelligible and inexplicable, associated with a trembling of the ground, – a rush and sweep of something through the air, like Death upon the wing. He shrunk, as if to let the thing go by. It was not gone, it never had been there, yet what startling horror it had left behind.[5]

The nameless fear recurs continuously, haunting Carker, robbing him of sleep and driving him as remorselessly as a similar compulsion had driven Bill Sykes, until he comes to the station, where it has a real existence:

> How long he sat drinking and brooding, and being dragged in imagination hither and thither, no one could have told less correctly than he. But he knew that he had been sitting a long time by candle-light, when he started up and listened in a sudden terror.
>
> For no, indeed, it was no fancy. The ground shook, the house rattled, the fierce impetuous rush was in the air! He felt it come up, and go darting by; and even when he had hurried to the window, and saw what it was, he stood, shrinking from it, as if it were not safe to look[6]

When the accident comes, the nightmare obsession is realised:

> He heard a shout – another – saw the face change from its vindictive passion to a faint sickness and terror – felt the earth tremble – knew in a moment that the rush was come –

uttered a shriek – looked around – saw the red eyes, bleared
and dim, in the daylight, close upon him – was beaten down,
caught up, and whirled away upon a jagged mill, that spun
him round and round, and struck him limb from limb, and
licked his stream of life up with its fiery heat, and cast his
multilated fragments in the air.[7]

The way Dickens uses the idea of the train in *Dombey and
Son* shows that he was thinking about the presence of forces
within and without the individual which were both vital and
destructive. But in *Dombey* we are aware of these forces only
accidentally. It is not part of the scheme of the novel to show
them working throughout life, but rather to show the psychological validation of the principles which Dickens founded
on them. In later novels – *Bleak House, Hard Times, Little
Dorrit* – these forces do come into prominence and are associated
with social factors such as Chancery, the Circumlocution Office
and the perverted power of machinery. In these novels Dickens
also identifies forces which are equally dangerous because they
do not allow for the actual nature of man – rationalism, psychology, political economy and social exclusiveness and
formalism. Yet while the social criticism develops, it never
usurps the place which is given to his anlysis of human
character and the general condition of mankind. In *Great
Expectations*, at this point when he returned quite consciously
to the autobiographical method he had used in *David Copperfield* and produced a work which totally reversed the social
optimism of the earlier novel, this is still clear. The critic of
the particular forms of nineteenth century society is aware
that the problem lies deeper than those forms, in human
nature.

The moral climax of *Great Expectations* is reached during the
courtroom scene in which Magwitch receives sentence of death.
Dickens uses again some of the techniques he had used in
'Ginshops', twenty five years before, but here they are fully
controlled and work in support of the novel's statement. He

conveys the vitality and variety of human action and reaction among the prisoners so as to heighten our awareness of the essential inhumanity of the ceremonious legal process:

> Penned in the dock, as I again stood outside it at the corner with his hand in mine, were the two-and thirty men and women; some defiant, some stricken with terror, some sobbing and weeping, some covering their faces, some staring gloomily about . . .
>
> The sun was striking in at the great windows of the Court, through the glittering drops of rain upon the glass, and it made a broad shaft of light between the two and thirty and the Judge, linking both together, and perhaps reminding some among the audience how both were passing on, with absolute equality, to the greater Judgement that knoweth all things and cannot err. Rising for a moment, a distinct speck of face in this way of light, the prisoner said, 'My Lord, I have received my sentence of Death from the Almighty, but I bow to yours', and sat down again. There was some hushing, and the Judge went on with what he had to say to the rest. Then they were all formally doomed, and some of them were supported out, and some of them sauntered out with a haggard look of bravery, and a few nodded to the gallery and two or three shook hands, and others went out chewing the fragments of herb they had taken from the sweet herbs lying about. He went last of all, because of being helped from his chair, and having to go very slowly; and he held my hand while all the others were removed, and while the audience got up, (putting the dresses right, as they might at church or elsewhere) and pointing down at this criminal or at that, and most of all at him and me.[8]

The touching presentation of the love which has developed between Pip and Magwitch is the central feature in this scene. Its moral quality is made explicit in Magwitch's humble reply to the judge and strengthened by the symbolic use of sunlight. Coming towards the end of the long process by which Pip has thrown off his egoism and his snobbery, breaking free of the social, and pseudo-moral, attitudes which prevented him from responding to the convict's coarse love, it completes the novel's implicit statement that humanity transcends the values imposed by society, by selfish craving for superiority and by the educated intellect. The novel reinforces this statement in various ways – most dramatically through the plot which reveals that the starlike heroine is the daughter of a convict and a murderess, and less directly through the portrayal of Miss Havisham, and the humorous juxtaposition of Jaggers and Wemmick.

Great Expectations, however, is not concerned merely to criticise organised society. It examines the nature of man and his position with respect to wider forces at work in life. Like so many of Dickens' novels it is concerned with the individual's vulnerability to exploitation through the affections. Miss Havisham's pathetic story brings this aspect most clearly to mind. She reacts to betrayal by instinctive withdrawal from experience and from a confession of even the most basic human needs, and with the simultaneous impulse to exploit mankind herself through Estella. The central story of Pip carries the theme through the whole novel. In the very beginning we are made aware, with brilliant economy, of the terms in which the child becomes aware of his identity. In effect, the opening scene of the novel presents Pip stripped of all the accessories which accompany identity – properly speaking he has neither name nor family. He is left to become aware of himself in becoming aware of the 'identity of things'. The paragraph in which he reports the way he acquired a consciousness of the world around him reflects the whole process by which the child's mind grows. His gaze gradually widens outwards, turning back with a new awareness of the existence of self which is also an awareness of weakness and physical misery :

> Ours was the marsh country, down by the river, within, as the river wound, twenty miles of the sea. My first most vivid and broad impression of the identity of things seems to me

to have been gained on a memorable raw afternoon towards evening. At such a time I found out for certain, that this bleak place overgrown with nettles was the churchyard; and that Phillip Pirrip, late of this parish and also Georgiana, wife of the above, were dead and buried; and that Alexander, Bartholomew, Abraham, Tobias and Roger, infant children of the aforesaid, were also dead and buried, and that the dark flat wilderness beyond the churchyard, intersected with dykes and mounds and gates, with scattered cattle feeding on it, was the marshes, and that the distant savage lair from which the wind was rushing was the sea; and that the small bundle of shivers growing afraid of it all and beginning to cry, was Pip.[9]

Magwitch's account of his own first awareness – significantly the point at which he begins the account of himself for Pip's bene- fit, stresses the same factors of loneliness and physical helpless- ness and shows the same concern for names. Magwitch also stresses the extent to which his part in life has been passive, and he the victim of physical and social forces acting in con- junction to exploit his weakness:

I've been done everything to, pretty well – except hanged. I've been locked up, as much as a silver tea-kettle. I've been carted here and carted there, and put out of this town and put out of that town, and stuck in the stocks, and whipped and worried and drove. I've no more notion where I was born than you have – if so much. I first became aware of myself down in Essex, a thieving turnips for my living. Summun had run away from me – a man – a tinker – and he'd took the fire with him, and left me very cold.

I knowed my name to be Magwitch, chris'ened Abel. How did I know it? Much as I knowed the birds' names in the hedges to be chaffinch, sparrer, thrush. I might have thought it was all lies together, only as the birds' names come out true, I suppose mine did.

So fur as I could find, there war'nt a soul that see young

Abel Magwitch, with as little on him as in him, but wot caught fright at him, and either drove him off, or took him up. I was took up, took up, took up, to that extent that I reg'larly growed took up.[10]

Even in his childhood view of Magwitch Pip confirms Magwitch's account of himself, and also shows the source of society's treatment of him in irrational fear of the irrational force he is thought to represent. Pip sees him as if reduced to the lowest and commonest elements, at once a helpless object and an object of fear:

A fearful man, all in coarse grey, with a great iron on his leg. A man with no hat, and with broken shoes, and with an old rag tied round his head. A man who had been soaked in water, and smothered in mud, and lamed by stones, and cut by flints, and stung by nettles, and torn by briars; who limped, and shivered, and glared and growled; and whose teeth chattered in his head as he seized me by the chin.[11]

Pip's first reaction to this figure is instantaneous fear, later qualified by sympathy, shared by Joe, which draws obscure signs of emotion from the convict himself. His relationship with Magwitch and the effect of this opening encounter, does much to form his whole character. Only much later can he shake off fear, and with it disgust, and relate to Magwitch in a simply human and affectionate way. His intermediate revulsion from Magwitch and the other convicts is a sign that he has assimilated the social and moral attitudes shown by other members of society towards himself as a child. Eventually he comes to associate coarseness, roughness and helplessness with love and humanity. At first, his ideas perverted by society's treatment of himself as a child, he practises dissociation. Later in life he looks back on his childhood persecution and sees it as naturally tending to produce the criminal mentality. Caught between the two sources of terror, Magwitch and his sister, one exploiting him in order to survive, the other through mere force of habit and domineering temperament, he is brought to the point when he is ready to commit any criminal act:

> Since that time, which is far enough away now, I have often thought that few people know what secrecy there is in the young, under terror. No matter how unreasonable the terror, so that it be terror. I was in mortal terror of the young man who wanted my heart and liver; I was in mortal terror of my interlocutor with the iron leg; I was in mortal terror of myself, from whom an awful promise had been extracted; I had no hope of deliverance through my all-powerful sister, who repulsed me at every turn; I am afraid to think of what I might have done on requirement, in the secrecy of my terror.[12]

What we learn through this encounter, and through the whole story of Pip's relationship with Magwitch, is that the sources of criminality are those very weaknesses in human nature which are most simply human and that, ironically, the more an individual seems merely human, the more fear he arouses in those around him. Pip himself experiences both the role of the passive victim and the role of the persecutor. Others, including Magwitch, Miss Havisham, and Estella herself, are forced into the same dual role. Society, with its false divisions and barriers, exacerbates the situation, but the evil seems to lie deeper, in the nature of human relationships, or in human character itself.

The contrast between *Great Expectations* and *David Copperfield*, in some respects the most similar of Dickens' works, brings out the very great range of tone throughout his fiction. *David Copperfield*, of all his novels, is the one we might refer to as most typically 'Victorian'. It certainly seems to some closer to observing the conventions and principles associated with Victorian Realism. It embodies a more positive and optimistic view of the condition of man in contemporary society than Dickens attempted in the work which preceded or followed it, and from the point of view of action and structure, approximates more closely to the quality and proportions of everyday life. In *David Copperfield* the metaphysical and moral problems which Dickens explores in all his fiction, from *Oliver Twist* to *Edwin Drood*, received a different treatment. As always, he is here concerned with the vulnerability of the innocent and good to exploitation and destruction, but the forms of evil are more natural. They are given causes in personality and environment and are deliberately kept within the scale of ordinary experience. The seduction of innocence takes the form of a natural event common in Victorian society, and is capable of expiation. Uriah Heep's wickedness is attributed to his training in charitable institutions, though not with complete consistency, and Mr Murdstone, who might well have been left with the awesomeness imparted by the child's uncomprehending view, is brought down to normal size in David's final meeting with Mr Chillip, and presented as the victim of his own religious ideas rather than as a monstrous exploiter of human weakness. The intrusions of evil which are not brought about by external means, such as the marital problems of Dr and Mrs Strong, are capable of direct treatment. Mr Dick's simplicity allows him to see beyond the issues which perplex them and restore their mutual confidence. It is as if Dickens had made up his mind to work out his deepest fears on the basis of a firm confidence in the nature of social life. Even the humorous characters, elsewhere condemned for ever to a limited state of being, can develop in this atmosphere to master themselves and their environment. Aunt Betsy, from the bizarre and aggressive figure that frightens Mr Chillip, changes visibly as she gains confidence in her relations with others and is freed from her encumbering husband. Mr Micawber, a more difficult case, is sent to breathe the freer air of the colonies. He is prepared for the new life, however, by his confrontation with Heep, which at once forces him back into himself, comically stemming his verbosity, and obliges him to recognise the existence of moral values and his relation to them. Most significant of all, Mr Peggotty shakes off the humorous characteristics which derive from his social situation and acquires dignity and self-consciousness.

Moving from *David Copperfield* to *Great Expectations*, we are aware of a substantial change of tone. This optimism has no place in the later novel. Yet the elements which make up the two images of life are essentially similar. As his career developed, Dickens' point of view changed radically, bringing within his reach, in the later years, a view which now seems fundamentally more 'realistic', stressing the elements of conflict and paradox in human character and situation. But when we turn to one of the greatest scenes in the earlier novel, comparing it with the later, the essential unity of his work becomes clear. The emphasis in *David Copperfield* is on resolution of stress, and ultimately the relief of distress; in *Great Expectations* we think rather in terms of the pain and sterility which is the price of understanding and love. The great storm scene in which Ham and Steerforth die before David's eyes, reminds us of the unity which lies beneath difference in tone and point of view. Steerforth and Ham, the seducer and the injured lover, their roles strangely intertwined as victim of the storm and would-be rescuer, affect, in the manner of their dying, the whole meaning of the novel. Brought together in death, without knowing it, their relationship dramatises precisely that connection between different elements of human nature that we find in *Great Expectations*. It is Dickens' great achievement that dramatic or narrative separateness and conflict can be used in this way, to imply a dimension of life which lies beyond the apparent reality in which his hero-narrator addresses the reader. The nature of this achievement is unique, but the essential principle is common to all Realist fiction – the energy which runs through all men, though distorted by vice, by social circumstances, or by ignorance and weakness, carries meaning and moulds experience itself.

11 *The History of Henry Esmond*: Thackeray's Anatomy of Sentimental Man

Thackeray's work stands out from mid-nineteenth century English literature by virtue of its strong vein of pessimism. He is unusual too, among Realist writers, in that he makes no attempt to give a metaphysical or spiritual dimension to the experience he depicts and has little faith in the individual's ability to understand life in general. His fiction forms part of the long-standing tradition, as old as the novel itself, in which human pretensions to freedom and dignity are subjected to harsh criticism. It is also part of the post-Romantic tradition in which the values most attractive to the writer, located within the individual's emotional and spiritual being, are dissected mercilessly and reduced in scale. It is easy to see Thackeray's work in relation to Flaubert's portrayal of Emma Bovary, or Frédéric Moreau, or the analyses of subjective egoism such as we find in Stendhal and de Musset. Yet Thackeray is closest of all to his English contemporaries. Before he became a critic of romantic ideals and sentiments, he was himself an idealist and sentimentalist, and his work, for all its subtlety of analysis and harsh criticism, asserts essentially the same values which are more absolutely asserted in Dickens, more optimistically in George Eliot.

Thackeray's writing career centres around his preoccupation

with the antithesis between actual and ideal. His view of life was coloured by the experience of disillusionment. As a sentimentalist, he was committed to the idea that meaning and happiness could be achieved only through emotional relations with other people, and that only a society which recognised this fact could be morally healthy. Yet he saw around him a society which perverted and stunted man's emotional nature, and he saw in the same glance that even the very source of life itself – man's emotional nature, was tainted. The individual facing life in Thackeray's work has to overcome disillusionment not only with external conditions, but with his own nature and with those nearest to him. Experiencing happiness only through love, he must accept love, mixed with jealousy, selfishness, possessiveness and irrationalism, as the source of unhappiness as well.

Thackeray's maturity begins at the point where this concern is introduced into his fiction as a central theme. Its introduction at a fairly late stage of composition transforms his 'Pen and Pencil Sketches of English Society' into *Vanity Fair*. The idea of life as a fairground, inhabited by people in pursuit of trivial ends, and the approach to his characters as puppets, both spring from the central idea that the moral disposition of his characters and their fate in the search for happiness are determined by their temperament, the circumstances of their upbringing and the lack of larger self-awareness. Becky Sharp and Amelia Sedley are presented against the narrator's conviction that happiness and even decency depend on emotional sensitivity. The novel's harshest criticism is reserved for those, like old Mr Osbourne, who will sacrifice others to their own pride and selfishness. Yet this very clear framework of values is fundamentally questioned by the novel's view of character. Becky, exposed to vice and misery at too early an age, reacts cynically and selfishly. In a sense, she would make a fit mate for Balzac's Vautrin. Yet Becky is on a smaller scale than Balzac's character, and is constantly thwarted by circumstances, by developments in other people, and by her own restlessness. Amelia has emotional susceptibility, but is lacking in self-criticism or the ability to evaluate other people. She is introverted, irrational and selfish. A mixture of passivity and stubbornness, she moulds her ideas of other people so as to make life accord with the demands of her temperament, and she is willing to destroy those closest to her in the process. The narrator, observing them both and seeing no one in the world around them who is capable of rising above the limited vision imposed by selfish craving, holds his own balance between cynicism and sentiment, precarious but persistent. In the world he presents, purity is impossible. But the weight in favour of emotional sensitivity is heavy. Innumerable instances reinforce his assumption – that if sentiment brings disillusionment mixed with happiness, cynicism brings nothing at all.

With *Vanity Fair*, Thackeray's basic attitudes were fixed, and the tone of his work remains constant, even though the angle of his view changed with each successive novel. In *Pendennis* (1848–50), he focuses on the moral and psychological problems that arise from the experience of disillusionment that comes with growth to adulthood in contemporary society. In *The Newcomes* (1853–5), he attempts a representation of the whole range of contemporary society, but centres the huge novel on the development of the individual's moral nature. *Henry Esmond* has a special place among his works, however, because it contains a closer and more intense examination of human character than Thackeray elsewhere attempted. It has been both his most popular and his most unpopular novel. Anthony Trollope called it the greatest of English novels,[1] and Harriet Martineau, not given to exaggerated praise, echoed the opinion of many when she referred to it as 'the book of the century, in its department'.[2] There were obvious reasons for this enthusiasm. *Henry Esmond* combined historical accuracy and authenticity, in an age when the synthesis of history and fiction represented the attainment of truth. For purists it combined consistency of tone with purity of style. It worked out its theme through direct action rather than reflection and comment, challenging

Scott on his own ground, without sacrificing sophistication. On the other hand, it seemed to many readers to cross the border between realism and cynicism. The remorseless accuracy of its analysis of sentiment, sexuality and moral impulses, disturbed contemporaries who needed a firm psychological basis for moral beliefs. And, perhaps most important of all, its representation of female character and love-relationships seemed to undermine the whole position of the sentimental morality central to Victorian culture.

Contemporary readers were also unsettled by the feeling that there was a close correspondence between the hero of the novel and the author; as Thackeray admitted, Esmond was a melancholy version of himself. Even now, the novel is difficult to interpret. It purports to be the autobiographical narrative of a man who has journeyed through life seeking happiness and understanding, and finding them in a retreat from the wider world, in romantic love:

> As I think of the immense happiness which was in store for me, and of the depth and intensity of that love, which for so many years, hath blessed me, I own to a transport of wonder and gratitude for such a boon – nay am thankful to have been endowed with a heart capable of feeling and knowing the immense beauty and value of the gift which God hath bestowed on me. Sure, love *vincit omnia*; is immeasurably above all ambition, more precious than wealth, more noble than name. He knows not life who knows not that: he hath not felt the highest faculty of the soul who has not enjoyed it. In the name of my wife I write the completion of hope, and the summit of happiness. To have such a love is the one blessing in comparison of which all earthly joy is of no value, and to think of her is to praise God.[3]

Difficulties arise from the fact that we learn – through the preface and through small incidents and hints scattered through the action – that the relationship between Esmond and Rachel was in fact far from perfect. We know that he was fiercely proud, formal even to those near him, and that she was fiercely jealous, even of her own daughter. We also have to balance this closing hymn to domestic bliss, which comes as an epilogue to the action, against remarks which Esmond himself has made throughout the novel, observations on the transience and shallowness of love and its dependence on temperament and personality. Finally, we have to reconcile Esmond's description of his happiness with Rachel with the fact that he experienced no romantic love for her before the point when he ends his memoirs, even when he knew that she loved him, and that he pursued her daughter, his first cousin, Beatrix, with passionate intensity. His second invitation to Rachel to come away to the New World with him, which she accepts, is seen to come logically rather than passionately, from a prematurely tired and disillusioned man.

These factors warn us that for all his apparent objectivity as narrator of his own history, Esmond is not to be identified with the author. Thackeray stands apart, pointing Esmond's deficiencies of judgement, temperament and knowledge. Yet the final effect of Thackeray's handling of the novel is to reinforce his hero's conclusion. *Henry Esmond* analyses the condition of love and the condition of the isolated individual in a harsh world. It shows love as a product of forces at work in the personality. Like all critical or 'realistic' fiction, it reduces absolutes. Yet it has the final effect, like all 'Realist' fiction, of showing emotional relatedness as the only source of happiness or meaning in human experience. Henry Esmond writes, at the end of his memoir, like a man who has made a great discovery of a truth which had lain near to hand all his life. The novel traces the process by which he came to make it and analyses the factors in his nature which prevented him from understanding it for so long.

Like Dickens' Pip, Esmond has no name, no family and no proper social position. As a bastard he bears the name of Esmond by favour and receives hospitality and education by charity. In his youth he experiences great loneliness, shows tenderness of nature and a need for affection and develops defensive pride, formality, and melancholy reserve. His first meeting with his mistress, Lady Castlewood, his cousin's young wife, brings all his childish feelings to one focal point. He experiences mixed love and worship for Rachel. She seems an angel, filled with divine pity and charity, and at the same time protecting with extended hand.

> Her heart melted, I suppose (indeed, she hath since owned as much), at the notion that she should do anything unkind to any mortal, great or small; for, when she returned, she had sent away the housekeeper upon an errand by the door at the farther end of the gallery, and coming back to the lad, with the look of infinite pity and tenderness in her eyes, she took his hand again, placing her other fair hand on his head, and saying some words to him, which were so kind, and said in a voice so sweet, that the boy, who had never looked upon such beauty before, felt as if the touch of a superior being or an angel smote him down to the ground, and kissed the fair protecting hand as he knelt on one knee. To the very last hour of his life, Esmond remembered the lady as she then spoke and looked – the rings on her fair hands, the very scent of her robe, the beam of her eyes lighting up with surprise and kindness, her lips blooming in a smile, the sun making a golden halo round her hair.[4]

Esmond tells us that this experience sends through his heart 'A keen and delightful pang of gratitude, happiness, affection . . .', so creating an association of ideas which is to affect him through his later life.

The years which immediately follow Esmond's reception into Rachel's family are years of innocent happiness. But as her marriage with Castlewood gradually breaks up Esmond is forced to witness the disintegration of affection, the process by which admiration and worship turn to scorn and bitterness and

hearty respect and rough affection degenerate to brutal indifference and drunken insult. His own helplessness in this
situation – 'compelled to understand and pity a grief which he
stood quite powerless to relieve'[5] – deepens his melancholy and
his tendency to world-weariness and cynicism. Involved in this
way, he is obliged also to witness, and even to take part in, the
series of events which lead to the duel between Castlewood and
Mohun, to be present at the death of his patron, and to learn
the deception which had been practised on him to keep him
ignorant of his own legitimacy. Esmond's reaction to his cousin's
deathbed confession is typical of him – he sacrifices his social
rights and indeed his whole social identity because of his emotional involvement with the family. As he burns the confession
he catches sight of the crude illustration on an ornamental tile
– Jacob cheating his father, Isaac. In effect his cousin has acted
the part of Jacob, yet Esmond seems himself to identify with
him rather than with Esau. Beatrix later refers to him as such,
waiting for Rachel. Ironically, he had been the very real cause
of the duel, because Castlewood had misinterpreted his wife's
alarm about Harry's well-being for concern about Lord Mohun.
Yet at this stage he is unconscious of the actual state of his
relationship with Rachel.

When Rachel turns on Harry during the scene in the prison
and blames him for Castlewood's death and her own unhappiness, her behaviour is the result of an hysterical reaction to her
realisation that her love has been transferred from her husband
to Esmond himself. Esmond, however, fails to realise this. Consequently he is overwhelmed by the bitterness of her attack
and his own sense of injustice. Her behaviour seems vicious
and irrational, and causes him pain which leave behind it an
indelible mark. The hand which protected and caressed has now
become a means of attack. His own hand is wounded and the
loss of blood from it when he misplaces his dressing brings the
unconsciousness which ends the scene. Esmond finds the
strength to endure his misery, turning further within himself,

but in later years he recognises that the sudden reversal from love to anger has left him permanently affected:

> You do not know how much you suffer in those critical maladies of the heart, until the disease is over and you look back on it afterwards. During the time, the suffering is at least sufferable. The day passes in more or less of pain, and the night wears away somehow, 'Tis only in after days that we see that the danger has been . . .
>
> O dark months of grief and rage! of wrong and cruel endurance! He is old now who recalls you. Long ago he has forgiven and blest the soft hand that wounded him: but the mark is there, and the wound is cicatrised only — no time, tears, caresses, or repentance can obliterate the scar. We are indocile to put up with grief however. *Reficimus rates quassas*: we tempt the ocean again and again, and try upon new ventures. Esmond thought of his early time as a noviciate, and of those past trial as an initiation before entering into life — as our young Indians undergo tortures silently before they pass to the rank of warriors in the tribe.[6]

A twelvemonth after the duel and his imprisonment Esmond returns from military service abroad with Marlborough's army because he has heard that Rachel is about to marry. He is consciously jealous, in spite of his resentment, by now aware of the fact that she is and will remain the central figure in his life.

Esmond and Rachel are reconciled at this stage; in the memory of the old man the act of taking her hand figures largely, symbolical of the restrained and qualified passion they experience.

> She gave him her fair hand, her little fair hand; there was only her marriage ring on it. The quarrel was all over. The year of grief and estrangement was passed . . . Brighter eyes there might be, and faces more beautiful, but none so dear —

no voice as sweet as that of his beloved mistress, who had
been sister, mother, goddess to him during his youth – goddess
now no more, for he knew of her weakness; and by thought,
by suffering, and that experience it brings, was older now
than she; but more fondly cherished as woman perhaps than
ever she had been adored as divinity. What is it? Where lies
it? the secret which makes one little hand the dearest of all?
Whoever can unriddle that mystery? . . . She took his hand
in both hers; he felt her tears. It was a rapture of reconciliation.[7]

The most interesting feature of this scene is that the rapture
remains merely one of reconciliation, although Rachel makes it
completely plain, and Harry realises, that she loves him passionately. Their roles are reversed. It is round his head now that she
sees a halo of sunshine, and her feelings are hysterically confused: 'She burst into a wild flood of weeping as she spoke; she
laughed and sobbed on the young man's heart, crying out wildly,
"bringing your sheaves with you – your sheaves with
you".'[8]

Esmond reports his own feelings as primarily wonder and
gratitude, and although he makes the offer, which Rachel
eventually accepts, of taking her to America, she refuses
because she realises that he does not love her as she loves him.
It is striking that Esmond is unable to respond to Rachael at this
stage. She is passionate, beautiful and deeply affectionate. But
at the very point of reconciliation between them – when
Esmond's love is beginning to deepen again – he turns away
from her and begins the long pursuit of Beatrix. Beatrix's starlike beauty inflames and enslaves him, even while he knows
that she is unattainable, that if she were attainable she would
be incapable of responding with affection; and while he tortures
Rachel by involving her in his courtship, Esmond rightly thinks
of his continuing infatuation with his cousin as a disease of
his nature from which he cannot escape but which marks him
for life. To gain her love he becomes a soldier, a man of letters

and a wit, and finally embarks on political adventure in the attempt to get the Stuarts restored to the English throne.

Even while he does this Esmond knows that Beatrix can never love him; that she would desert him for a man she could love; that marriage with her could never bring happiness. The nature of his love, however, is conditioned by his character. His love for Rachel seems to exclude sexual desire. He speaks of it as if it were already fulfilled, remarking on the difference between his feeling for the two women: 'Is memory as strong as expectancy? fruition as hunger? gratitude as desire?'[9] His love for Beatrix, on the other hand, which is strongly sexual, is also associated with ambition and the attempt to obtain a social position. It is interesting to notice that this passionate love, so long continuing, dies on the spot when he reads the note she has left for the Prince – not, surely, because it tells him something about his mistress which he did not know, but rather because his personal honour is touched. His bitter resentment at her behaviour is not caused by sexual jealousy, strongly felt before, but by outraged honour. Significantly, his response to the Prince's attempt to seduce Beatrix is to break his sword, renounce his allegiance, and burn the papers which proved his legitimacy. The effect of this action is to create a scene where he appears more noble than the King, drawing the allegiance of the only subject present, his cousin Frank. The logic of his action derives from his personality. Esmond's personal honour represents his identity; any infringement of that causes him to retreat within himself. That retreat is symbolised by the sacrifices of his claim to a social identity and demands from others a respect reserved for purely moral qualities.

Looking back through Esmond's account of his life, we notice that similar scenes feature strongly. The first sacrifice at the deathbed of Lord Castlewood, Frank's father, is followed by repetitions of the same idea – all of which help to draw the kind of mingled love and admiration on which Esmond seems to thrive. When Rachel learns of his action from the old Viscountess her reaction is to fling herself at Esmond's feet and to kiss both his hands 'in an outbreak of passionate love and gratitude, such as could not but melt his heart'. His action extorts the response which he has previously given her before, as he puts it, he learns her weaknesses:

> 'Don't raise me,' she said, in a wild way to Esmond, who would have lifted her. 'Let me kneel – let me kneel, and – and worship you.'[10]

Through Rachel the announcement is made a third time for the benefit of Beatrix and the Duke of Hamilton, whose response is a dignified recognition of Esmond's nobility of spirit: 'To be allied to you, sir (so his Grace was pleased to say), must be an honour under whatever name you are known'.[11]

Esmond's air of modesty and genuine self-criticism cannot conceal the fact that he suffers from a passionate, introverted pride which continues to the end of his life. Esmond needs not only love, but admiration. He extorts it unconsciously by the noblest possible self-sacrifice. For the greater part of his active life, in the Old World, he is incapable of experiencing sexual passion and affection together. His experience of love has perverted his nature, added to the need for defence which his bastardy and loneliness created in the first instance. Significantly, he feels desire for the only person in his immediate circle who refuses to be subordinated by admiration, and loses this when her behaviour threatens the basis of his self-respect. Esmond is truly noble, but not absolutely so. He attains nobility by virtue of the fact that he feels deeply and recognises the nature of his feelings, and acts accordingly in ways that are morally appropriate. On the other hand, his self-sacrifice is but a product of his pride, and that itself, like his melancholy pessimism, is the result of the instinct for self-protection. Ironically, Esmond protects himself too well – protects himself from love, by separating it from desire and externalising desire itself. Consequently he is unable to recognise what Beatrix, for all her waywardness, sees clearly – that he and Rachel love each other and could live happily together. In the end that happiness comes to him only as the result of accident. Nothing has happened to change the central characters, but there is an end of the conditions which have kept them apart. Esmond proposes to Rachel once again – this time to rescue her from domestic inconvenience. His language includes no note of passion: 'It was after a scene of ignoble quarrel on the part of Frank's wife and mother . . . that I found my mistress one day in tears, and then besought her to confide herself to the care and devotion of one who, by God's help, would never forsake her.'[12] He promises constancy but not passion. He had been taught by his own experience that love does not last, that passion is no more than a disease or personal inclination; at a deeper level, beyond his own consciousness, he had been incapable of giving and receiving on equal terms. In his marriage with Rachel, to his gratitude and surprise, he discovers this ability within himself. Fiercely proud to the end, but protected from the world within his relationship with Rachel, Esmond learns to love and be loved, and gains a happiness not merely the only happiness, but one which is supreme.

It is interesting to speculate on what the creators of Frédéric Moreau of *L'Education Sentimentale,* or Sir Willoughby Patterne of *The Egoist,* would have made of Esmond's type of morbid egoism. Thackeray is kinder to his hero than Flaubert or Meredith would have been. Close to Esmond himself, he concentrated on the nature of Esmond's consciousness and the implications of his development and his discovery. They would rather have tended to examine the nature of the consciousness in the moment of moral decision, or the effects of egoistic pressures on the hero and on those who surround him. Yet the friction of all three authors is closely connected. Flaubert stands apart from the English novelists in so far as he is more pessimistic and more critical of the modern consciousness. Even so, he analyses and dissects human character, as they do, from the point of view of someone who has dreamt of a human world where love could be absolute and pure. English writers of this period never abandon their faith in the possibility of reconciling the vision and the reality in some degree. To criticise sentiment and yet to maintain a sentimental morality, a belief that in man lay man's happiness, was first the achievement of Thackeray, but after him of other writers within the expanding tradition of Realist fiction.

12 George Eliot: the Philosophy of Realism

Readers who were still young in the 1880s lived into a time when it was necessary to explain George Eliot's enormous contemporary reputation. Those who sought to do this described how she had seemed in comparison with her rivals to offer a broader and deeper view of humanity and human character, to combine philosophy with religion and humanity – as Richard Hutton put it, to 'see and explain the relation of the broadest and commonest life to the deepest springs of philosophy and religion'. So Oliver Elton explained:

I recall without apology the fervid, overcharged view of George Eliot. She was a sybil; she read the surface and the depths alike infallibly. *Middlemarch*, above all, was an image of life; and if it was a gloomy one, so much the worse for life . . . And the writer had her own consolations, though not of the ordinary kind. She had cast off the current doctrines; she had managed to 'do without opium'. The 'religion of humanity', the voices of the 'choir invisible', sounded in the ear, though their comfort was of a far-off and grimmish order. And then George Eliot had, or so it appeared, unique claims as a writer. Dickens often 'sat on the piano'; Thackeray (I still cite the headlong immature notion) was apt to maunder, and had no philosophy or sense of beauty; the experience of the Haworth sisters was intense but limited.

But George Eliot's canvas was broad, her ideas were broader still; her people were alive and real, and innumerable; and the play of motive in her tales, the course itself of the action, revealed the spiritual issues that shape even the humblest fates.[1]

Elton's description is not far removed from the terms which occur in early enthusiastic reviews of Eliot's work; it reflects the aspects of her writing which contemporaries found most impressive and shows the way in which certainly G. H. Lewes, and very probably Eliot herself, thought of her relationship with contemporary novelists.

It is difficult not to think of George Eliot's novels as representing the maturity of the novel in the period after Scott; only in her novels was the balance between ideal and real, subjective and objective elements of experience, the balance between poetry and science or reason and religious faith, confidently and consistently struck. Contemporaries saw in her work a developing control over elements typical to English literature and fiction in all periods and especially the literature of their own time. Eneas Dallas compared her with Austen, pointing out how she excelled the former in more difficult subjects, 'with wilder passions, with stronger situations, with higher thoughts'. Dallas also observed the similarity between Eliot and Thackeray in their fundamental humanism, but showed how she was different in the greater positiveness and benevolence of her approach.

We do not mean for one moment to detract from Mr. George Eliot's originality when we say that after his own fashion he follows this difficult path in which Mr. Thackeray leads the way. He has fully reached that idea which it is so easy to confess in words, but so hard to admit into the secret heart, that we are all alike, that our natures are the same, and that there is not the mighty difference which is usually assumed between high and low, rich and poor, the fool and the sage, the best of us and the worst of us . . . But . . . Mr. Eliot is

good enough to tell us that we have all a remnant of
Eden in us, that people are not so bad as is commonly
supposed and that every one has affectionate fibres in his
nature . . .²

Though she denied discipleship to Thackeray, Eliot's admiration
for him went a good way, but she went far beyond his work
for inspiration, back to romantic poetry and fiction. She clearly
thought of Wordsworth's poetry as standing behind her own
work, and drew directly on the examples it provided of the
interfusion of the humane and the spiritual. Walter Scott's
novels, though she at one time wondered at his spiritual darkness, were like a mine of crude materials to be more finely
worked. Even at the end of her career, when she came to work
out the characterisation of Mordecai in *Daniel Deronda*, it was
to Balfour of Burley in Scott's *Old Mortality* that she turned
for a reference to a cruder version of the type she was concerned with. It was to Scott too, however, that Eliot owed, as
she later confessed, the first moments of doubt that eventually
led to the complete abandonment of orthodox Christianity. This
makes it doubly significant that her associations with his writings were so emotional that she could not bear to hear him
criticised. The association of the first impulses towards
rationalist criticism, with the moving pictures of humble life
and character, is typical of the basic link in her mind between
the sentiment of humanity and the impulse to rationalist
criticism that later formed the guiding principle in her thought
and conditioned her whole view of art.

The timing of George Eliot's career as a novelist is something
more than the accident of biography. Among the major novelists
of the first two-thirds of the century she alone had gone
through the religious crisis we often think of as typically
Victorian. But instead of declining into scepticism or finding
some new basis for accepting orthodoxy, she was able to transfer
religious and spiritual values to human experience itself.
Marianne Evans's long period of religious enthusiasm and

religious doubt had educated her in the techniques of rationalism and in the methods of higher criticism; her association with Spencer and Lewes and her continuing education gave her a grounding in the techniques of experimental science. So far her position had much in common with that of Harriet Martineau, whose education in a shallower rationalism led her eventually to throw off religious faith and seek in human experience, viewed scientifically, the truth she was emotionally equipped to demand. But Harriet Martineau, in the final analysis, was unable to rest in uncertainty, or to find that certainty outside the scientifically provable. Eliot was able to do this. She found refuge in the religion of humanity, the proper expression of which was in the art that expressed, objectively and imaginatively at one and the same time, the total view of contemporary experience.

In enabling George Eliot to do this, positivism played an important part, together with other movements leading to an increased tendency to treat human character and activities as ends in themselves. But Martineau, too, had the opportunity to study the works of Comte. The fundamental difference between them is the tendency of George Eliot to make final reference to imaginative experience, and her ability to think her way through to a position from which life could be positively analysed and seen as a whole. Martineau had begun to do this. In her attempt to combine Scott's achievement with Jane Austen's she had sketched out the territory which her greater successor actually covered. The failure of the one and the success of the other is obviously a matter of the difference between two individuals, but it is also something more. Twenty years before 1856 religious humanism was an impossibility – so must also have been the type of novel which gave it expression.

It was the larger view that her position in time made possible that enabled George Eliot to make the decisive step of giving philosophic, moral and religious value to the 'extension of sympathies' which literature brought about. The new perspective created by mid-century developments in geology, biology and anthropology, permitted the reconciliation of morality, necessarily based on freedom of the will, romanticism, demanding the recognition of a spiritual element in human experience, and the principle of determinism, implied in scientific and rationalist thought. To George Eliot the essence of rationalism and the 'supremely important fact' was the 'reduction of all phenomena within the sphere of established law', which depended not on abstract theorising, but on practical sciences:

> The great conception of universal regular sequence without partiality and without caprice – the conception which is the most potent force at work in the modification of our faith, and of the practical form given to our sentiments – could only grow out of that patient watching of external fact, and that silencing of preconceived notions, which are urged upon the mind by the problems of physical science.[3]

The application of these principles to the study of the history of the human race revealed, as Eliot describes in an approving review of R. W. Mackay's *The Progress of the Intellect*, 'that divine revelation is not contained exclusively or pre-eminently in the facts and inspirations of any age or nation, but is co-extensive with the history of human development . . .' The passage which follows, in Eliot's account of Mackay's faith, is a clear indication of the basis of her own creed:

> The master key to this revelation, is the recognition of the presence of undeviating law in the material and moral world – of that invariability of sequence which is acknowledged to be the basis of physical science, but which is still perversely ignored in our social organization, our ethics, and our religion. It is this invariability of sequence which can alone give value to experience and render education in the true sense possible. The divine yea and nay, the seal of prohibition and of sanction, are effectually impressed on human deeds and aspirations, not by means of Greek and Hebrew, but by that inexorable law of consequence, whose evidence is con-

firmed instead of weakened as the ages advance: and human duty is comprised in the earnest study of this law and patient obedience to its teaching . . . In this view religion and philosophy are not merely conciliated, they are identical: or rather, religion is the crown and consummation of philosophy – the delicate corrola, which can only spread its petals in all their symmetry and brilliance to the sun when root and branch exhibit the conditions of a healthy and vigorous life.[4]

Taken in conjunction with the idea of progress or moral evolution, this idea of the law of consequence provided Eliot with a means of reconciling the rival schemes of social and individual morality current in her day – orthodox Christianity and Benthamite utilitarianism. The Benthamite aim of individual happiness and self-fulfilment could be linked to the Christian conception of universal love in the new humanitarianism, which looked on self-development and emotional fulfilment as the means by which the largest moral aims could be achieved.

In Eliot's thinking the ideas implicit in much of early nineteenth century English fiction and poetry become explicit. Her view of life permitted her not only to reconcile determinism and free will, but to make the limitations of human nature and the human condition the basis of a new assertion of purpose and dignity in human life. The contemporary novel as it had developed throughout the century was a perfect instrument for the expression of this view. It could describe the individual in society and in the material world as the focal point of external forces, and at the same time present internal experience and development in time, relating external circumstances with moral development. It could combine analysis and affirmation, showing their essential relationship. Her ideas about fiction represented a new development, but a natural and inevitable development. She might be said to draw out the central principles embodied in the fiction of Dickens and of Thackeray and, with a more detached intellectual viewpoint than either, to integrate them successfully.

In Eliot's view, a view greatly influenced by Dickens, the supreme importance of fiction lay in its capacity to extend human sympathies and thus to forward the central moral principle of the modern world, acting in behalf of the highest religion:

> Art is the nearest thing to life – it is a mode of amplifying experience and extending our contact with our fellow men beyond the bounds of our personal lot.[5]

This sympathy, however, is dependent on a true understanding of human nature. Fiction which presents an unreal or inaccurate view of the human condition, or of human character, stultifies the end of morality and religion, preventing readers from perceiving the laws which govern and limit them. This is the reason why Eliot criticised Dickens, very much as Thackeray had done, in spite of her great debt to him:

> We have one great novelist who is gifted with the power of rendering the external traits of our town population; and if he could give us their psychological character – their conceptions of life and their emotions with the same truth as their idiom and manners, his books would be the greatest contribution Art has ever made to the extension of social sympathies. But . . . he scarcely ever passes from the humorous and the external to the emotional and tragic, without becoming as trancendent in his unreality as he was a moment before in his artistic truthfulness. But for the precious salt of his humour which compels him to reproduce external traits that serve in some degree, as a corrective to his frequently false psychology, his preternaturally virtuous poor children and artisans, his melodramatic boatmen and courtesans, would be as noxious as Eugene Sue's idealised proletaires in encouraging the miserable fallacy that high morality and refined sentiment can grow out of harsh social relations, ignorance, and want; or that the working-classes are in a condition to enter at once into a millenial state of altruism, wherein everyone is caring for everyone else, and no one for himself.[6]

In her earliest fiction, *Scenes from Clerical Life* (1856), she sets out to demonstrate that the human sympathy which Dickens' fiction embodies can be understood in the world around us only by the reader who is content to do without idealism, sentimentalism and sensation.

> The Rev. Amos Barton, whose sad fortunes I have undertaken to relate, was, you perceive, in no respect an ideal or exceptional character, and perhaps I am doing a bold thing to bespeak your sympathy on behalf of a man who was so very far from remarkable, – a man whose virtues were not heroic, and who had no undetected crime within his breast; who had not the slightest mystery hanging about him, but was palpably and unmistakeably commonplace . . . Yet these commonplace people – many of them – bear a conscience, and have felt the sublime prompting to do the painful right: they have their unspoken sorrows, and their unspoken joys; their hearts have perhaps gone out towards their first-born, and they have mourned over the irreclaimable dead. Nay, is there not a pathos in their very insignificance – in our comparison of their dim and narrow existence with the glorious possibilities of that human nature which they share.
>
> Depend upon it, you would gain unspeakably if you would learn with me to see some of the poetry and the pathos, the tragedy and the comedy, lying in the experience of a human soul that looks out through dull grey eyes, and that speaks in a voice of quite ordinary tones.[7]

Criticism here works to restore a sense of proportion, a sense of reality – but beneath this is the implicit faith in the dignity of human nature. The heroic and sublime ideal is humanised within the realist novel.

Eliot continued to develop her ideas about realism in *Adam Bede*, where she challenges the aesthetic which defines beauty in primarily formal terms. In Realist fiction as she defines it beauty and truth are identified with sincerity or feeling: 'All honour and reverence to the divine beauty of form! . . . but let

us love that other beauty too, which lies in no secret of proportion, but in the secret of deep human sympathy'.[8] But in
practical terms she was developing far faster. In *Scenes from
Clerical Life* the drama is subdued and the focus is directed on
to the blend of triviality and partiality with nobility and sensitivity in human character. In *Adam Bede* the focus is thrown
on to the action and the moral view of the narrator is justified
through psychological analysis of the internal experience of the
characters. A new shift is given to the patterns previously
established in nineteenth century fiction. For the basis of her
plot Eliot went to Scott's *Heart of Midlothian,* which examines
the working out of the law of consequences externally, against
the background of the Porteous riots in eighteenth century
Scotland. Eliot sets the action of her novel in the English
countryside in the later years of the same century and shifts
the emphasis from external events to internal development in
her characters. Hetty Sorel and Arthur Donnithorne, the
equivalents of Scott's Effie Dean and Stanton, learn through
bitter experience the inevitable results of indulgence in passion
in defiance of circumstances. Adam, Eliot's central character,
has a lesson of sympathy and understanding to learn. He is
helped by Dinah, whose Methodism Eliot presents as a crude
means of combining sympathy, spirituality and self-restraint.
These outlines of this moral scheme, worked out in the central
action, are softened by the element of humour in the characterisation, and through the comic and sympathetic view of the
determining and limiting factors of social life.

Yet in spite of a much greater overall success, *Adam Bede*
fails in the same way as Harriet Martineau's *Deerbrook,* in its
presentation of the psychological development of its central
characters. Neither Dinah nor Adam quite succeed in playing
the parts designed for them. The dramatic events following
Hetty's flight and leading up to her transportation draw our
interest from the process by which Adam should be seen to
become a sadder and a wiser man, and his eventual union with
Dinah lacks psychological as well as dramatic interest. It was

only with *The Mill on the Floss*, her second novel, that Eliot overcame this difficulty and succeeded in developing all the central aspects of her subject matter. In *The Mill on the Floss* the tendencies implicit in the nineteenth century English novel as a whole are taken a stage further. In particular, the tensions and preoccupations most central to the Victorian novel are brought out more self-consciously and brought closer to reconciliation and integration than before had been possible.

The Mill on the Floss brings to full development that interest in the conditions affecting human character which characterises all earlier nineteenth century fiction. Eliot achieves this by embodying the conditioning elements concretely, in family and social relationships, and in the stages and modes of individual growth, showing their effect on the fully developed character. In the drama which centres on character development, external incident and internal reaction are completely integrated. Her point of view is that of the biologist or sociologist. She writes of human life as if it were capable of being objectively and scientifically analysed. Yet her interest is primarily moral. The individual's moral sensibility is seen as the highest aspect of his development, and moral attitudes of society as the result and representation of its physical, economic and intellectual condition. She avoids determinism by virtue of her sensitivity to the elements which work in human nature in spite of conditioning. She presents these as constantly evolving and gradually coming to be more fully understood and embodied in social and religious forms.

The tragic action of *The Mill on the Floss* arises from the fact that its central characters – 'in the onward tendency of human things' – have risen above the mental level of the generation before them, and yet by virtue of the sensibility that enabled them to develop, have been tied to those around them 'by the strongest fibres of their hearts'.[9] The novel presents a society which is materialistic and narrow, showing English provincial life at a time when the nation as a whole was more in-turned and conservative than at almost any other period. The moral strength and oppressive narrowness of the middle classes are embodied in the Dodsons. In the Tullivers, the paternal branch of Tom and Maggie's family, there is an element of passion and imagination which finds no socially approved outlet. Mrs Moss, Tulliver's sister, has married poorly, for love, and earns the disapproval of those for whom material respectability is the primary moral concern. Tulliver himself, lacking education or refined self-consciousness, gives vent to his passionate nature only in the feud with Wakem. His moral conceptions are crude, but vigorous. The lawyer represents the devil, vengeance is a sacred duty to be imposed on those who follow him. Achieving it himself in horsewhipping his opponent, he exhausts himself and dies, pathetic in his ability to understand the world around him: 'This world's . . . too many . . . honest man . . . puzzling . . .'

Maggie and Tom inherit from both sides of the family, though nature and circumstances develop their characters in different ways. Tom's 'education' at the hands of Rev Walter Stelling prevents him from acquiring any acquaintance with ideas and experiences which might have opened his mind. When he comes to manhood suddenly, after his father's collapse, his vigorous and passionate nature finds no course but to follow the narrow, crudely moralistic ideas of the Dodsons, which seem to have been justified by his father's downfall. With an energy and intensity characteristic of the Dodsons, he succeeds in clearing his father's debts and repossessing the Mill, but at the same time he becomes incapable of understanding his sister, gets further turned in on himself as a result of his complacent priggishness, and by the end of the novel is completely isolated.

Maggie escapes Tom's fate because as a girl she is kept at home rather than given an expensive education. Shielded from the world, and left very much to her own devices, she develops an active imagination which grows side by side with a developing moral sense. Her softer nature enables her to be more sensitive to others and yet it involves her in an immature commitment to Philip Waken which inevitably causes trouble in the family, and which is based on no real affection on her side. At the same time she seeks in Christian resignation and sacrifice the fulfilment of natural but crude impulses of an 'undisciplined heart'. In the writing of Thomas à Kempis she discovers a new world of experience which she seeks to enter without trial or the test of long suffering:

> With all the hurry of an imagination that could never rest in the present, she sat in the deepening twilight forming plans of self-humiliation and entire devotedness; and, in the ardour of first discovery, renunciation seemed to her the entrance into that satisfaction which she had so long been craving in vain. She had not perceived – how could she until she had lived longer? – the inmost truth of the old monk's outpourings, that renunciation remains sorrow, though a sorrow borne unwillingly. Maggie was still panting for happiness and was in ecstasy because she had found the key to it.[10]

Maggie's later meeting with Stephen Guest shows her a different kind of world. With Stephen she could find happiness of a different sort, in emotional and sexual fulfilment. But by this time circumstances, relationships and her own actions have woven a net of commitment from which she cannot break, because her whole moral and personal development has taken place within it. In leaving Stephen and returning to St Oggs, in spite of his grief and bitterness, and in spite of the fact that she has lost her good name entirely, Maggie is accepting her own moral responsibility for her situation. She reaches a higher stage of development than Tom. His relatively crude victory over economic circumstances is compared with her far more painful victory over her own character.

The ending of *The Mill on the Floss*, some critics have thought, should have come when George Eliot had made this point clear. The later sections of the novel certainly lack fulness of development, as Eliot herself was aware. On the other hand, to think of them as hurried or ill prepared is to miss the novel's central point. Though Henry James was drawn to question whether the dénouement 'was a tardy expedient for the solution of Maggie's difficulties', Eliot had planned the flood and the death of Tom and Maggie from the beginning.[11] Their reunion in the face of physical danger is in fact not a means of escape but the way Eliot chooses to complete the novel's statement. The flood, for those who live near the banks of the Floss, is a continuing threat from year to year – a reminder to the reader of man's helplessness before nature and of his essential vulnerability. The instinctive love which brings Maggie to Tom's rescue, and which brings the childish words to Tom's lips in the moment of danger, is the element in human nature which lies deeper than all the factors of opinion, attitude, conviction which keep them apart. Earlier in the novel, as she introduced us to the town of St Oggs, Eliot told us about an earlier flood in the legendary past of the town. The town itself she sees 'as a continuation and outgrowth of nature', a work of man which reflects every stage of his history, showing at once the passage of time and the persistence of his natural patterns of behaviour. Into this description, not without some humour, she inserts the story of Ogg, the son of Beorl, a ferryman on the river in the times before history began, who recognises the need of a poor woman and rows her across on a night of storm.

> Still she went on to mourn and crave. But Ogg the son of Beorl came up and said, 'I will ferry thee across: it is enough that thy heart needs it.' And he ferried her across. And it came to pass, when she stepped ashore, that her rags were turned into robes of flowing white, and her face became bright with exceeding glory . . . And she said – 'Ogg the son of Beorl, thou are blessed in that thou dist not question and wrangle with the heart's need, but wast smitten with pity, and didst straightway relieve the same . . .'[12]

This legend, which has given the town its name, means more to Eliot than a reminder of the 'visitation of the floods'. It also extends our understanding of the view of human nature she is presenting, preparing us for what is later to happen in the flood which engulfs Tom and Maggie. Here, in legendary form, we see the awareness in past generations of the element of love which transcends material considerations, recognised as the deepest element of human nature, unaffected by the continuing development of moral conceptions and attitudes, or by the circumstances which inhibit, stunt and destroy the individual man or woman.

The Mill on the Floss is Eliot's first mature work because it is the first novel which embodies the confident and positive expression of her essentially sentimental view of human nature, together with the concrete representation of the limiting and conditioning factors which make up the element in which we live. It is also the first of her novels in which she develops the capacity to analyse individual character so as to show the developing relationship between circumstances, inherited characteristics, emotional impulses and moral views. It establishes the framework within which she worked for the remainder of her career. *Middlemarch* is a better constructed novel than *The Mill on the Floss* and presents a more complex view of the relationships between temperament and circumstances and between individuals within a self-contained society. *Daniel Deronda* is concerned with the present and with the future development of society rather than the recent past, like most of her other novels. But all Eliot's works remain within the framework set up in *The Mill on the Floss* – and this is closely related to the work of her contemporaries and immediate predecessors. Eliot's central characters must all learn essentially what Maggie learnt, passing through the same temptation to indulge in idealism and egoism, risking the sterility which comes with egoism, and finding fulfilment only through the discipline of their emotions. The acceptance of pain, the need for resignation, the possibility of failure and bitterness such as comes to Lydgate or to Gwendolen Harleth is always set side by side with the meaningfulness which can follow an understanding of the fact that freedom is achieved by accepting the factors and impulses which shape and limit our nature from within. Henry James would have preferred a novel called 'Gwendolen Harleth' rather than *Daniel Deronda*, but in the balance of the two cases and in the fact that they are intimately tied together, lay George Eliot's essential aim as a novelist.

13 George Meredith: the Novelist as Internal Historian

While George Eliot published *Daniel Deronda*, George Meredith was bringing out some of the best of his long series of novels. During the 1870s he won very little popular support, but gradually built up a reputation among young artists and intellectuals. After the publication of his first collected edition in 1886, the pace accelerated. His *Diana of the Crossways* for the first time had something of a wide popularity. By the 1890s his fame was established at what has since seemed an incredibly high level, beyond the comprehension of many reviewers. By that time he was felt as a positive force in contemporary society, as an intellectual who made his fiction the vehicle of an advanced and sophisticated analysis of culture and society, and as an artist whose work combined exciting new experiments in technique and material and yet seemed to preserve, from an earlier stage of the novel's history, a correspondence with the inner principles of life itself. After 1885 it was difficult to escape Meredith's influence. H. G. Wells, for one, was strongly affected, and the confession of one of his modern heroes shows what freshness and immediacy of impact Meredith could achieve, even in his seventies:

A book that stands out among these memories, that stimulated me immensely, so that I forced it upon my companions, half in the spirit of propaganda, and half to test it by their comments, was Meredith's *One of Our Conquerors*. It is one of the books that have made me. In that I got a supplement and corrective of Kipling. It was the first detached and adverse criticism of the Englishman I had ever encountered. It must have been published already about nine or ten years when I read it. The country paid no heed to it, had gone on to the expensive lessons of the War because of the dull aversion our people feel for all such intimations, and so I could read it as a book justified. The war endorsed its every word for me, underlined each warning indication of the gigantic dangers that gathered against our system across the narrow seas. It discovered Europe to me, as watching and critical.[1]

One of Our Conquerors must have had a similar impact on many young readers between 1891 and 1914. Meredith's was one of the few intelligently critical voices raised at this time and in support of his insistent demand for a national self-criticism, presented an analysis of contemporary life which was severely honest and penetrating.

Even during Meredith's life, however, there were critics who could see that his great modernity amounted to nothing more than a brilliant adaptation of a criticism which was really based on principles that belonged to earlier generations. As Percy Lubbock said, immediately after Meredith's death: 'In art his aims are no longer ours, nor in life perhaps his creed . . .'[2] Less perceptive commentators praised Meredith because he 'solved the problem of contemporary literature half a century before it existed'. At this distance, however, we can see that the problems he actually solved were not in fact those of contemporary literature. The problems he addressed himself to are accurately summarised in one of the obituary articles:

How to present a view of life both wise and brave, answering to experience as well as to desire, serviceable in art or the daily walk? Single in essence, in appearance they are manifold: How to give pleasure without corrupting the heart, and how to give wisdom without chilling it? How to bring into

G*

play the great passions of men without unchaining the beast? How to believe in Darwin and the dignity of man? How to believe in the nerves without paralyzing the nerve of action? How to recognize the weakness of man, and not forget his heroism . . . How to believe that evil is fleeing forever before good, but will never be overtaken and slain? How to look back upon a thousand defeats, and yet cling to the fighting hope. If you look through this list of questions you will not find one which Meredith did not answer.[3]

This is true; but it must also be said that these were not the questions which preoccupied those younger artists of the period who have since come to seem truly modern. All the questions in the list reduce to one basic question: how to preserve a belief that life is meaningful in circumstances which seem to deny it? This was what preoccupied Thackeray, Clough, George Eliot and Arnold, but not Henry James – nor Joseph Conrad, Yeats, James Joyce; these later writers were conscious of new problems and new forces at work in contemporary society, of which Meredith was aware, but to which he responded in a different fashion. When these problems rose to the surface, after the First World War, then Meredith's reputation, like that of Browning, deflated rapidly to a point well below its right level. Only then did the critics realise that his attitudes were those of earlier decades and dead generations.

Meredith's mind was formed in the years before and after the European revolutions of 1848. The great event of the century to him was the realisation of Mazzini's dream in the unification of Italy. Unlike the writers we commonly think of as most typical of the mid-Victorian period Meredith escaped from what J. B. Priestley refers to as the 'Science/Religion, Idealism/ Materialism trap'.[4] Educated abroad at the Moravian school of Nieuvied, in his early years more open to the influence of Romantic poets, to Scott and Goethe, then the theologians and essayists at work in England, he threw off the remains of orthodox religion without difficulty or residual guilt and was free to take on the task of applying the principles of Romanticism directly in a modern environment. In his youth Meredith echoes the tenets of the Romantic poets. 'Yes!' he wrote in the columns of an amateur magazine, 'the Universe is but a succession of lives and we are all united – in nobility – and gentleness and love. All that is brutish is also of kin – but gentle love uniteth all.'[5] His own experience of gentle love in the disastrous marriage with the daughter of Thomas Love Peacock helped to educate him further. In the decade between his marriage and the publication of *Richard Feverel* he had developed a philosophy in which not love, but Law, was prominent. Maturity brought him to an awareness of the extent to which human freedom is restricted – not primarily through the determining influences of place and time but those which are created by our own past actions, which weave a net of circumstances and habits around us and give rise to endless chains of causality which, thoughtlessly prepared, often have the effect of trails of gunpowder leading to an unforseen but inevitable explosion. As with George Eliot, a close reading of Romantic poetry, of Goethe and Scott, helped to create in Meredith's mind a residual confidence in the meaningfulness of life in spite of the operation of law. Contemporary ideas of evolution helped him too, to create a philosophy in which rationalism and idealism were reconciled. At bottom this philosophy rested on the rejection of subjectivity and selfishness, and the individual's acceptance of the working of forces set in motion by previous actions of his own. The idea of race development and the principle of evolution helped Meredith to see the willing acceptance of this determinism as the true source of human freedom. The key to human progress and to individual fulfilment lay in the individual's intelligent understanding of his own relationship with the universe and his firm control of the baser element of his own nature. Clear-sighted acceptance of nature is the first step in the development of the Meredithean character; this is followed by an awareness of his own limitedness and the foolishness which is the inevitable lot of man in whom primitive egoism, under many masks, is the strongest impulse, driving him forward, possibly upward, if subject to the right controls.

One of the principal means by which civilised man could ensure the development of the individual and society along the right lines, Meredith thought, was comedy, which he described as a spirit which casts a humanely malign glance on aberrations from right reason, or proportioned, intelligent behaviour among men. Meredith's view of comedy looms perhaps too large, however, at a time when he is read primarily through the *Essay* and *The Egoist*. For him art was of primary importance because it was a means by which man could understand the whole of life. It could embody not only material law, but also the immaterial aspect of experience, its special province. At the end of his long life he told a friend: 'Chiefly by that in my poetry which emphasises the unity of life, the soul that breathes through the universe, do I wish to be remembered, for the spiritual is the eternal.'[6] Even in his *Essay*, where Molière receives great praise as the exponent of pure comedy, Shakespeare and Cervantes are brought in to show that there is a great art which is not social or even critical. Though Shakespeare 'is a well-spring of characters which are saturated with the comic spirit', 'they are of the world enlarged by our embrace by imagination, and by great poetic imagination'.[7] Cervantes' case proves for Meredith that the intelligently critical does not reach the borders of art. In his distinction between comedy and Cervantean humour there is something of the qualitative distinction common in mid-Victorian definitions. The humorist, according to Meredith, may lack the comic virtues of balance and *mesure*, but when he has genius he achieves 'an embrace of contrasts beyond the scope of the comic poet'.[8]

The writers whom Meredith recognised as masters in their art were great because they mounted from a firm basis of realism to a higher vision, combining an understanding of the laws working on man with a capacity for realising his spiritual potential. They combined realism and idealism: 'they give us earth, but it is earth with an atmosphere'.[9] As a critic Meredith praised realism wherever he found it; he commended the Pre-Raphaelites for naturalness and accuracy, and condemned others for their lack of vivid realisation, or 'want of truth'. Flaubert's *Madame Bovary* he commended for moral truthfulness and because 'all is severe matter of fact, painfully elaborated', without 'the old blandishing graces' of Dumas, Balzac and Sand.[10] Yet Meredith also attacked the naturalism of the Zolaesque type as strongly as he assailed the 'rose-pink' idealism of the Tennysonian *Idylls*. Realism was the proper basis of art, but idealism was necessary. As he put it in 1856, 'the tendency of art is to excellence and that of the spirit to idealism. It will not for ever walk the earth and pore on nature. It has the quality of flame once kindled'.[11]

Thirty years later, in *Diana of the Crossways*, Meredith was reasserting these principles. He criticised the new naturalist fiction coming from France, regarding it, at its best, as a corrective to 'rose-pink' idealism. In place of both, he recommended 'Philosophy', which reflected the balance between spiritual and physical elements in human nature:

Then, ah! then, moreover, will the novelist's Art, now neither blushless infant nor executive man, have attained its majority. We can then be veraciously historical, honestly transcriptive. Rose-pink and dirty drab will alike have passed away. Philosophy is the foe of both, and their silly cancelling contest, perpetually renewed in a shuffle of extremes . . . will no longer baffle the contemplation of natural flesh, smother no longer the soul issuing out of our incessant strife. Philosophy bids us to see that we are not so pretty as rose-pink, not so repulsive as dirty drab; and that instead of everlastingly shifting those barren aspects, the sight of ourselves is wholesome, bearable, fructifying, finally a delight. Do but perceive that we are coming to philosophy, the stride toward it will be a giant's – a century a day. And imagine the celestial refreshment of having a pure decency in the place of sham; real flesh; a soul born active, wind-beaten, but ascending.[12]

Art without philosophy, in Meredith's eyes, becomes 'the pasture of idiots, a method for idiotizing the entire population which has taken to reading.'[12] Philosophy in fiction, on the other hand, is a means of clothing the skeleton of truth with solid flesh 'humanly shapely'.[13]

To do this was Meredith's object. The primary means to it, he thought, was through the incorporation of 'brainstuff', by transferring attention from external events and conventional characterisation to internal action, so that the fiction be moulded on the inner skeleton of a subject probed to the centre. If he could do this, he rightly thought that he would have brought about a revolution in fiction which none of his predecessors had either ability or courage enough to perform. Thackeray had come close, but had failed:

A great modern writer, of clearest eye and head, now departed, capable in activity of presenting thoughtful women, thinking men, groaned over his puppetry, that he dared not animate them, flesh though they were, with the fires of positive brainstuff. He could have done it, and he is of the departed! Had he dared, he would (for he was Titan enough) have raised the Art in dignity on a level with History, to an interest surpassing the narrative of public deeds as vividly as man's heart and brain in their union excel his plain lines of action to eruption.[14]

For Meredith, to be a novelist was also to be an 'internal historian,' keeping his predecessors' sharp observation of external mannerism and action, but interpreting them always as signs of what was going on inside the character.

Almost from his earliest beginnings as a writer, the essential framework of thought which conditioned Meredith's view of fiction was complete. So with his first prose fiction he encountered the fundamental problem of reconciling the two separate aspects of his artistic purpose – representation of processes of growth and development in individuals, and incorporation of an overall criticism of life as a whole. In *The Shaving of Shagpat* (1856), this is done through a loose allegory, centring on the preparation of the race-hero, Shibli Bagarag, for an heroic task. Shibli rises from the rank of humble barber to shave the hairy Shagpat and free the human race from the illusion that society should be based on the absolute supremacy of a king-figure attributed with mysterious power. Before he can achieve this task he has to go through a painful series of tests which chasten his egoism and make him aware of his own position in the universe, surrounded by forces that he can use, but not dominate. Eventually he achieves clearness of vision and an indestructible sense of proportion, instilled by his many beatings, and he is fit for the great task. All Meredith's later heroes go through much the same process, though rarely with such amusing success as Shibli. The qualities he attains – self-discipline, stability, patience, and a confirmed faith in the immaterial dimension of experience – are those which we learn to appreciate in all Meredith's novels.

Meredith's first novel, *The Ordeal of Richard Feverel*, presents a case where the hero fails in the task of self-development, gives way to crude egoistic impulses and brings disaster on himself. In the history of English fiction *Richard Feverel* represents an appreciable step forward. Together with the sonnet series, *Modern Love*, it marks the abondonment of orthodox moral and aesthetic categorisation and the development of the subject according to its own inner logic. *Richard Feverel* relates the natural development of a young man protected from the chastening experiences which crudely organised society prepares for its youth, by a father who determines to bring him up entirely on a determinist system of education. At a crucial point the father's own personal weakness causes him to step aside and release control, in resentment at the course which the youth quite naturally takes, and Richard heads for catastrophe like a bullet from a gun. Without the self-awareness and experience that normal life would bring, the fundamental innocence and freshness of feeling his protected life has given him are dangerous qualities. The novel ends when the consequences of the mode of education, followed by the father's inevitable loss of control, are worked out. The conclusion is bleak – Richard, recovering from fever, has to face life with the knowledge that his headstrong impetuosity has killed his young wife. Experience withheld has forced itself on him at a price too high for any-one to pay.

Richard Feverel is a brilliant novel, quite widely recognised as such at the time of publication, but it was by no means completely coherent.[15] The positive import of the corrective case Meredith intended to show was that a proper bearing towards life would permit his characters to avoid the disastrous combination of chance and impulse which destroys Richard. In the view of life which is quite clearly implied in the novel determinism and human freedom are compatible. But in this novel, which sprang directly, and no doubt at the price of great personal conflict, from his own experience as a husband and father, Meredith confusingly distributed various of the elements at work in life in general among characters in the action. So the philosophy of determinism, which sees man as machine, is represented by Sir Austen, the cynical view which calls for compromise and manipulation at every crisis by Adrian Harley, his own attitude by Richard's other cousin, Austen Wentworth. When first published the novel also contained a good deal of digressive comic material which undermined the serious analysis of life, and the most understanding reviewers rightly complained that essential points were needlessly obscured.

In later work Meredith set out to develop his view of character, further clarifying his ideas of the laws governing life and the relation between the forces at work in personal relations and society at large. This involved him in a degree of purely intellectual experimentalisation which alienated readers won by his earlier work and reduced his effectiveness as a novelist. A sense of aesthetic proportion was never Meredith's strong point and the need to work out a purely intellectual scheme as he went along reduced it further; public stupidity about his work confirmed him in isolation. It was only with the novels he produced after this period of self-discovery that he reached the level of *Richard Feverel* again, and then as the result of a deliberate effort to work within the framework created by other writers.

This central point in Meredith's career is marked by the publication of *The Adventures of Harry Richmond*. None of the novels published between this work and *Richard Feverel* had been well received; nor were any of them sufficiently successful in integrating experimentation in character portrayal and structure with the full realisation of a human situation to deserve wide popular acclaim. In *Sandra Belloni* (1864) he dealt primarily with the forces at work in the development of individual character, studying the contrasted lovers, Emilia Belloni and Wilfrid Pole and trying to relate the story of their relationship to wider social criticism through connected action and the study of socially representative groups. In *Vittoria* (1866) he followed the adventures of the same heroine, but shifted the focus of his attention radically by subordinating the development of individuals to a study of the development of Italy at one of its most formative moments in the struggle for union and independence. In *Rhoda Fleming*, published in the same year, he reduced the social level of his characters, tried to show the 'laws of life' in operation at a lower social level and in a more domestic plot. All three novels show radical deficiencies in composition and proportion. Their highly intellectual plotting is never completely related to the narrative interest generated by the action.

The Adventures of Harry Richmond was Meredith's last bid for a widely based popularity. It also came at the point when he had for the first time fully mastered his own ideas. Both these factors contributed to his decision to work within an established fictional mode. Though the germs of the story seemed to demand a treatment combining the burlesque picaresque, and the satirical, *Harry Richmond* as it developed in Meredith's mind, became an autobiographical *Bildungs-*

roman, in which the elements of social criticism, the survey of Britain's cultural position in contrast with that of Germany, and the presentation of psychological and social analysis, were subordinated to the narrative of Harry Richmond's development from childhood to manhood, maturity, and marriage. In effect, *Harry Richmond* is a reworking of *David Copperfield*. Motherless Harry is also deprived of a stable father; dumped at school, he forms friendships with the Traddles-type innocent, Temple, and with Heriot, a less powerful version of Steerforth. Kiomi, Harry's childhood gipsy companion after his escape from boarding school, falls victim to Heriot. Harry survives his childhood experiences, his wanderings through London and the Continent, his disappointed dream of marrying a real princess, to settle down with his cousin Janet, accepting his own limitations and her mundane but admirable virtues and taking a firm position within the society that his madcap father sought to dominate.

The novel's central concern is with the development of the hero, but its interest is greatly deepened by the fact that Harry is subject to two contrary influences, represented by characters of great humour – the ebullient pretender to royal blood and princely rank, his father, Richmond Roy, and the irascible, powerful and affectionate old man, his grandfather. The two, in mortal rivalry for Harry's affections, are fully humorous characters, passionate and vital to the point of madness in their different ways, careless of what they destroy in the process of attaining the end immediately dictated by passion or fantastic ambition. Another profoundly humorous character, the sea-captain, Welsh, a scaled-down, comic version of Captain Ahab, sails the North Sea seeking for souls in peril, risking destruction at the hands of an unreliable crew, through sheer inability to see beyond the melodramatic vision of retribution that fills his mind and dominates his whole view of the world. Harry himself, at the risk, as Meredith realised, of being made to seem too weak a character, is subject to pressures created by these characters, but they exist in the world reflected in his adventures as totally independent characters, whose own adventures go to make up the total understanding of life which the hero has achieved by the time he writes his narrative.

In *Harry Richmond*, in fact, the attraction of the *bildungsroman* to Victorian authors is more clearly evident than usual. It provided an opportunity, in the first place, for a full account of individual development from ignorance to understanding of the world, which could be expected to force itself on the conviction of the reader as he read, much as it had forced itself on the understanding of the hero as he lived. At the same time, with some influence from the picaresque, it provided an opportunity for the introduction of a wide range of characters and groups of characters, whose own situations and stories could be made to demonstrate the same laws. The integration of these separate aspects of interest on the superficial level of biography could be given greater depth and authority by means of systems of images and the use of symbolic events and references. In this respect *Harry Richmond* is especially notable. The richer texture and greater solidity of realisation which bring it closer into line with other mid-Victorian novels partly conceal the fact that Harry's narrative is equipped with a complete and closely interwoven system of imagery, strengthened and given absolute value by incidents which carry out into the 'real' world implications which would otherwise only exist on the level of metaphor. Behind Harry's narrative there is an analysis of life, the elements of which have been broken down and presented in terms of natural imagery. This system of imagery must be considered not as the creation of an author but as the spontaneous discovery of each of the characters, the unconscious revelation of the hero-narrator, rather than a device which he is using.

Harry Richmond is thus Meredith's most 'Victorian' novel, presenting a reconciliation of determinism and freedom through restraint of selfish impulses and integration with life as a whole, on the social and spiritual levels, showing the same principle at work in a larger dimension and using the structure of the fiction to dramatically inter-relate the two areas of interest. So it is essential to the understanding of Meredith's relation to his period and to the tradition of Realist fiction in which he actually worked, although his technical experiments created a superficial appearance of a more radical departure from convention. His next novel, considered in relationship with *Harry Richmond*, explains the basis of his later popularity, in the capacity to adapt his philosophy and artistic purpose to new areas of experience, to carry further the logic of his own development, and to achieve a new kind of penetrating and yet coherent criticism of contemporary life on the basis of principles as old as the work of his master Goethe.

Meredith's own description of *Beauchamp's Career* is accurate and illuminating:

> It is philosophical – political, with no powerful stream of adventure: an attempt to show the forces around a young man of the present day, in England, who would move them, and finds them unutterably solid though it is seen in the end that he does not altogether fail, and has not lived quite in vain. Of course, this is done in the concrete. A certain drama of self-conquest is gone through, for the hero is not perfect. He is born of the upper class and is scarcely believed in by any class, except when he vexes his own, and is then to be hated . . . I think his History a picture of the time – taking its mental action, and material ease and indifference, to be a necessary element of the picture.[16]

Meredith's subject has two dimensions; the hero against England and the hero against himself. These two elements in Nevil Beauchamp's headlong 'career' are skilfully interwoven by the narrator. The events in Beauchamp's personal development are seen in the context of his political activity; and we see him decline from his self-chosen status as epic hero in proportion as he rises towards the status of fully developed social man. The narrator's view of the subject is deeply ironical, underlining the discrepancy between Beauchamp's apparent heroic potential and his actual achievement in the domestic circle. Yet in spite of this deflationary concern, the novel is strongly assertive of merely human values. Man in *Beauchamp's Career* is defined in terms of his limitations, but the attainment of self-understanding is presented as the result of a struggle more truly heroic and far more difficult than that involved in the Byronic assertion of self against circumstance.

The Byronic hero – 'that conqueror of cirmumstances' – is of no interest to Meredith. He chooses rather to deal with a 'hero whom circumstances overcome', and his narrator claims a rigid impartiality and determination to portray the real rather than the imaginary – to portray the actual conditions of life without evasion or distortion:

> I give you the position of the country undisturbed by any moralizing of mind. The youth I introduce to you will rarely let us escape from it . . . and our union is one of which, following the counsel of a sage and seer, I must try to paint what is, not that which I imagine. This day, this hour, this life, and even politics, the centre and throbbing heart of it (enough, when unburlesqued, to blow the down off the gossamer-stump of fiction at a single breath, I have heard tell); must be treated of men, and the ideas of men . . .: these are my theme; and may it be my fortune to keep them at blood heat, and myself as calm as a statue of Memnon in prostrate Egypt . . . I can at any rate be impartial.[17]

Nevil Beauchamp, whose mind and personality we are shown being formed under the influences of English culture and aristocratic society, throws himself with passionate energy against the apathy of Englishmen, in the fight for radical reform of society. He meets inevitable defeat, and at the same time, and for the same reasons, loses the woman he loves and gradually comes to see as the fit companion in a life of patriotic devotion to radical politics. But the loss of Cecilia and the subsequent dangerous fever of the hero is followed by a recovery and marriage with the perhaps more suitable Jenny Denham, which brings to Beauchamp for the first time something of the sense of proportion and restraint previously lacking. When Jenny

and Nevil return from a cruise at sea after the first months of
marriage, the hero has gone a good way to completing a difficult education and understanding the relationship of the individual with society as a whole, his comparative insignificance and
the inevitable slowness of political change and development.
At this moment, which might well mark the ending of the
Victorian *bildungsroman* and corresponds closely to the point
at which *Harry Richmond* comes to an end, there is a sudden
and disastrous invasion of change. Rowing up-river from the
yacht, Beauchamp is involved in a boating accident. He dives
to save a child, recovers him, returns to rescue the child's
brother and is drowned.

E. M. Forster, misunderstanding the novel's harsh realism,
remarked about its ending: 'there is an attempt to elevate the
plot to Aristotelian symmetry, to turn the novel into a temple
wherein dwells interpretation and peace'.[18] The striking quality
of Meredith's realism is the degree to which it can persist in
spite of the absence of symmetry and peace, though the confidence in interpretation remains throughout all. Meredith ends
the novel by presenting the scene on the river bank as the two
old men, at one time in sharp and brutal opposition to one
another and now united in love for Nevil, the nephew of one,
adopted stepson of the other, look at the child he has saved:

All the lights of the ring were turned on the head of the boy.
Dr. Shrapnel's eyes and Lord Romfrey's fell on the abashed
little creature. They boy struck out both arms to get his fists
against his eyelids.
This is what we have in exchange for Beauchamp!
It was not uttered, but it was visible in the blank stare at
one another of the two men who loved Beauchamp after they
had examined the insignificant bit of mudbank life remaining
in this world in the place of him.[19]

Nevil's death is the natural result of his impetuous nobility, his
leading characteristic throughout his short life, but there is no
attempt to make this a fit ending to his career. The complete

silence of the narrator at this point rather brings out the extent to which Meredith means us to see this brutal invasion of chance as an element of experience which is inexplicable. Pitted against the apathy of the English, or against the forces of nature – tiredness, cramp – Beauchamp is defeated.

The novel offers no compensation for the grief of the old men – no humanitarian gesture to reduce the sense of loss. With Beauchamp a force working for nobility, generosity and sheer vitality, has gone out of existence. The loss is absolute. Yet at the same time, *Beauchamp's Career* suggests that the life and death of the hero leave unaffected the possibility of understanding human experience. The real achievement of Beauchamp survives death precisely because it is unheroic – not a victory over circumstances, which change, but an impact on human nature, which does not. Beauchamp's death repeats the pattern of previous action – a great deal is given for an apparently small return, but a human return, which is not amenable to crude and confident measurement of the kind which the reader is likely to demand. Beauchamp's failure to be a hero, as his uncle the Earl of Romfrey points out, was a failure only in unimportant terms:

'He hasn't marched on London with a couple of hundred thousand men: no, he hasn't done that,' the Earl said, glancing back in his mind through Beauchamp's career . . . 'No! we haven't had much public excitement out of him. But one thing he did do: he got me down on my knees!'

Lord Romfrey pronounced these words with a sober emphasis that struck the humour of it sharply into Rosamund's heart, through some contrast it presented between Nevil's aim of the world and hit of a man: the immense deal thought of it by the Earl, and the very little that Nevil would think of it – the great domestic achievement to be boasted of by an enthusiastic devotee of politics.[20]

Meredith's own career, far from headlong and very long-lasting, was a strange one. In 1856 when he began writing, he seemed revolutionary, yet actually built his work on the same basic underlying principles which shaped the work of his successful contemporaries. By 1896, when he was still writing, he was accepted as a sage and prophet, the leading intellectual and artist of his time. By then his work was actually outdated. *Beauchamp's Career*, which exactly marks the mid-point in this career, shows the exact nature of his contribution – the great openness which be brought to Victorian fiction, the degree to which he forwarded the development of internalisation, created a vocabulary and methods for the investigation of levels of experience his predecessors ignored or censored out, and, above all, came closer than earlier English novelists to representing identity in a moving present, rather than a fixed fictional past. On the other hand, *Beauchamp's Career* also shows the degree to which he remained a 'Victorian' in spite of his rejection of moralistic or sentimental values, inhibitions and restrictions. In all his work, as the very fundamental principle of his thought, he sought for meaningfulness, unity and coherence, he sought a means of reconciling what in the Victorian context were felt as conflicting elements of experience – nature and law, circumstance and freedom, scientifically based truth, and the truth of the emotions, the passions and the spirit of man. These principles conditioned the range and the shape of his novel's; they limited his freedom, and at the same time produced the most distinctive and rewarding quality of his work.

Conclusion
The New Realism:
Henry James's 'Straight Path'

From Dickens to Meredith, Victorian fiction hangs together, constantly developing, but doing so within a firm and well defined framework, itself an important factor contributing to the great achievement in English fiction at this time. From the 1870's on, however, the development of principles implicit in Victorian culture was taken to an extent which inevitably led to the destruction of this characteristic framework. The result was a further radical shift, accompanied by a mingled sense of achievement and loss and complicated by the fact that it brought about the decisive breach between audience and artist which had held good from the time of Walter Scott. The central principle motivating artists at this time was itself derived from Romantic principles passed down through Victorian literature – especially the idea that it was primarily through imaginative art that truth could be established. But in the later decades of the nineteenth century, subject now to French and Russian influences, English writers sought to discard or transcend Victorian conventions and limitations and to establish through literary experiment, or through naturalistic reproduction of experience, the truths that Victorianism obscured. The novels of Thomas Hardy reflect this process at a deeper level, but it is clearly working in the fiction of George Moore, of George Gissing, of H. G. Wells, and Arnold Bennett.

At this point, in fact, we see the beginnings of modern literature, decisively marked off from the great Victorian period. These latest years of the century are a period of transition, which yet possesses its own certainties, its own permanent achievement, and which justifies a detailed study in itself. Nevertheless, a narrower focus is possible. We have been concerned with the faculty with which the novelist shapes experience into fiction and with the structural qualities of his work. And this preoccupation directs us clearly to Henry James, rather than to Hardy, Gissing or Moore, as the writer who most eminently possessed this shaping faculty himself and was most conscious of its changing role at the time when he lived. Transition in literary history, though gradual in its working, must appear abrupt. In between two novels a revolution may be seen to have taken place. So wherever we place the beginnings of modernism, and however keenly we are aware of the co-existence of factors derived from the past, or pointing to the future, in James's *Portrait of a Lady* we must realise that we are faced with something fundamentally different from anything that precedes it.

James's debt to those who preceded him – to Dickens and Eliot, Thackeray and Meredith – was immeasurable, but for all that he owed to their tradition, he departed from it fundamentally. *Portrait of a Lady* is based on a value system closely similar to that of Eliot and her predecessors – juxtaposing moral and emotional sensitivity with materialism, formalism and selfishness. The complex image and symbol system of the novel instructs us as to the connection between emotional sensitivity and the capacity for moral response. It not only condemns the hardened, materialistic egoism of Osmond, but mocks the heroine's egoistic dreams of freedom, and ends by asserting, in realist fashion, the essential connectedness between all human beings. Isabel must – like Maggie Tulliver or Clara of *The Egoist* – eventually recognise that her identity consists in the relationships and responsibilities which she has created for herself. Yet the novel is fundamentally different from those which precede it.

The nature of the difference becomes very clear at the end of the novel. In technical terms it is innovatory, abondoning the types of closed fiction typical of the Victorian novelists, avoiding explicitness and presenting the action very directly. The reader has to analyse for himself the terms in which the experience is reported to have presented itself to the central character. The reason for this is that James is suggesting that the process of decision which takes place within his heroine is not simply a moral one, and is outside the grasp of the conscious mind. Isabel's identity, she has come to understand, is not absolute, but consists in relationships, memories, habits of mind and strong emotional impulses which are beyond her control. In the climatic scene with Goodwood at Gardencourt, after Ralph's death, she has to go along a path prepared for her by her own actions which she can find only after a confused and disturbing emotional experience. We understand what is happening to her only when we realise that the series of image references which have been built up throughout the novel and given psychological validation in the report of Isabel's experience and the description of other characters, is being suddenly reversed. Our expectation through the later part of of the novel is that she will somehow turn away from the sterile relationship with Osmond and find freedom, light and self-fulfilment in some other relationship, which offers love and sensitive responsiveness. Though Goodwood has not seemed to offer such an alternative at earlier stages, Isabel is surprised at this point to discover that she can now respond to the sexual relationship he offers, which presents itself in terms which have previously been thought of as morally good – refreshing moisture and light. In James's account of her response to his embrace, however, the images open out, taking on other aspects, which are destructive. After the kiss Isabel knows that freedom and self-fulfilment lie, for her, outside the relationship with Goodwood, and even in the prison-like atmosphere which Osmond has created within their marriage:

Isabel gave a long murmur, like a creature in pain; it was as if he were pressing something that hurt her . . . The world, in truth, had never seemed so large; it seemed to open out, all round her, to take the form of a mighty sea, where she floated in fathomless waters. She had wanted help, and here was help; it had come in a rushing torrent. I know not whether she believed everything he said; but she believed just then that to let him take her in his arms would be the next best thing to her dying. This belief, for a moment, was a kind of rapture, in which she seemed to beat with her feet, in order to catch herself, to feel something to rest on . . . He glared at her a moment through the dusk, and the next instant she felt his arms about her and his lips on her lips. His kiss was like white lightning, a flash that spread, and spread again, and stayed, and it was extraordinarily as if, while she took it, she felt each thing in his hard manhood that had least pleased her, each aggressive fact of his face, his figure, his presence, justified of its intense identity and made one with this act of possession. So she had heard of those wrecked and under water following a train of images before they sink. But when darkness returned she was free . . . She had not known where to turn; but she knew now. There was a very straight path.[1]

From the technical point of view, this is a very striking passage, but its primary importance does not lie in this. What James does here is very closely related to the work of his predecessors – and some of them, like Meredith for example in *The Adventures of Harry Richmond*, are equally capable of presenting crises of identity by similar means. In contrast, however, to Meredith's work, and in even more striking contrast to that of George Eliot, James presents Isabel as turning away from sexual or pronouncedly emotional experience, and makes no attempt to give her experience any social or metaphysical content. *Portrait of a Lady* compares closely in some respects with Eliot's *Daniel Deronda* and Meredith's *Diana of the Crossways*, which also study the development of character in a wider and deeper sense than was previously done in Victorian fiction. But in both those novels there is an attempt to make a meaningful relationship between the development of the individual heroine and the circumstances of life in general – she is presented in relation to material, psychological and moral laws which are themselves related one to another, and her life is presented as meaningful in the extent to which she understands and accepts them. James's study, by contrast, is far more absolute. The terms in which Isabel comes to understand her own identity are hers alone, and they lead her not towards an understanding of life in general and an integration with it, through her emotional nature, but into a strangely and ironically narrow, darkened world, which is the only place she can actually live with that degree of sensitivity brought to her by painful experience of her own mistakes. This is realistic, perhaps, but it is not Victorian Realism. With James the barrier has been crossed. The laws within which the English novelists operated, from Scott to Meredith, no longer apply. The result is a new sense of freedom, the removal of restrictions and the escape from the ever-present danger of hypocrisy and reticence. The price paid for this was the loss of a solid yet flexible framework, into which the novelist could assimilate themes, patterns and situations from science, from social studies and from other forms of literature, and which gave him a means of presenting what it felt like to be alive in his period, and of commenting on, analysing and explaining the meaning of life as a whole.

Notes

INTRODUCTION

1 See, for example, J. F. C. Harrison, *The Early Victorians, 1832–1851* (1971) p. 57.
2 E. Heller, *The Disinherited Mind* (1952, Penguin ed., 1961) p. 42.
3 'On Love' (1815?); *Selected Poetry, Prose and Letters*, ed. A. S. B. Glover (1951) pp. 974–5.
4 The time-lag between England and Germany in this respect was observed by Carlyle in his *Life of Schiller* (1825); see Centenary Ed., ed. H. D. Traill, xxv pp. 46–7.

PART I   THE ENGLISH NOVEL IN THE ROMANTIC PERIOD

1 J. M. S. Tomkins, *The Popular Novel in England, 1770–1800* (1832) p. 1.
2 This widely current view of fiction can be found almost anywhere the novel is discussed throughout the eighteenth century, but one of its very earliest proponents was the famous Bishop Huet, in his essay *Sur l'origine des Romans* (1670). An English version is reprinted in the present writer's *Novel and Romance, 1700–1800, a documentary record* (1970).
3 *Rambler* 4, 31 Mar 1750.
4 'An enquiry into Those Kinds of Distress which excite Agreeable Sensations', *Miscellaneous Pieces in Verse and Prose*, J. and A. L. Aikim (later Mrs Barbauld) (1773). See also *Novel and Romance*.
5 H. Cockburn, *Memorials of His time* (1856) pp. 45–6.
6 *New Monthly Magazine*, I (1821) 393–403.
7 Rev. E. Mangin, *Essay on Light Reading* . . . (1808) p. 50. See also H. Murray, *Morality of Fiction; or, An Inquiry into the Tendency of Fictitious Narratives* . . . (1817). Murray is more liberal than Mangin, thinking it 'improbable that so universal an inclination should be altogether of a vicious and hurtful nature, or that there should not be some useful purposes which it is destined to serve.' The reader still interested after studying these two essays might well

go on with Harriet Kiernan's Royal Irish Academy prizewinning *Essay on the Influence of Fictitious History on Modern Manners* (1815) – a turgid summary of all the current platitudes.

8 'Letters of Julia and Caroline', *Letters for Literary Ladies* (1796) p. 3.

The Novels of Jane Austen

1 A. W. Litz, *Jane Austen: A Study of Her Artistic Development* (1965) p. 3.
2 Ibid., p. 143.
3 By Professor R. Pascal (see below, note 15).
4 *Emma*, ed. R. W. Chapman (1933) pp. 136–7.
5 Ibid., p. 142.
6 Ibid., pp. 375–6.
7 Ibid., p. 429.
8 Ibid., p. 26. The italics, of course, are mine.
9 Ibid., p. 34.
10 Ibid., p. 482.
11 Ibid., p. 149.
12 Ibid., p. 408.
13 Ibid., pp. 411–12.
14 *Pride and Prejudice*, ed. R. W. Chapman (revised ed., 1965) p. 208.
15 R. Pascal, *The German Novel* (1956) p. 3.

The Novels of Walter Scott

1 Frederick Denison Maurice's remarks form part of an excellent criticism he produced in his early days as editor of the *Athenaeum*, No. 14 (14 Mar 1828). Carlyle's more famous criticism of Scott appeared in his review of Lockhart's *Life* (*London and Westminster Review*, 1838); see Centenary Ed., xxix.
2 *The Two Drovers* (1827); Centenary Ed., xx pp. 343–4.
3 Ibid., p. 349.
4 Ibid.
5 The quotation here is from Alexander Welsh's illuminating discussion in *The Hero of the Waverley Novels* (1963) p. 58.
6 *Waverley* (1814); Centenary Ed., I p. 36.
7 Ibid., p. 57.
8 Ibid., p. 296.
9 Ibid.
10 Ibid., p. 346.
11 Ibid., p. 375.
12 Ibid., p. 392.
13 Ibid., p. 153.
14 Ibid., p. 92.
15 Ibid., pp. 154–5.
16 Ibid., p. 282.
17 Ibid., pp. 342–3.

18 Scott was quite aware of the deficiencies of his own work, of course. His *Quarterly Review* (XVI, 1817) essay is among the best criticism of his novels. See also *Sir Walter Scott on Novelists and Fiction*, ed. I. Williams (1968) p. 237.

19 'Death of Lord Byron', *Edinburgh Weekly Journal* (1824); *Miscellaneous Works*, Library Ed. (1878) I p. 435.

PART II   ROMANTIC TO VICTORIAN

1 A. W. Benn, *The History of English Rationalism in the Nineteenth Century* (1906) p. 368.

2 L. E. Landon, *Romance and Reality* (1831) p. 98.

3 Sir S. E. Brydges, *Sir Ralph Willoughby; An Historical Tale of the Sixteenth Century* (1828) preface.

4 That is, *Saint Leon* (1799); *Fleetwood: or the New Man of Feeling* (1805); *Faulkener, a Tragedy in Prose* (1809); *Cloudesley, a Tale* (1830); *Deloraine* (1835).

5 *The Literary Life of John Galt* (1834) p. 26.

6 *Autobiography* (1833) p. 219.

7 *The Literary Life*, p. 24.

8 Ibid., p. 229. This is the principal which guided Galt in his best work – 'to bring impressions in the memory harmoniously together. . . .'

9 'On Novels and Novel Writing', *Metropolitan Magazine*, V (1832) 235.

10 Ibid., p. 236.

11 *De Clifford, Or, The Constant Man* (1841) pp. 254–5.

12 E. Bulwer Lytton, *England and the English*, 2nd ed., 2 vols (1833) p. 94.

13 A. K. Tuell, *John Sterling. A representative Victorian* (1941) p. 242.

14 M. M. Waddington, *The Development of British Thought from 1820–1890* (1919) pp. 61–2.

15 *England and the English*, pp. 106–7.

16 This point has been well made by Louis Cazamian; see *Le Roman Social en Angleterre* (1831–50) (1934; repr. New York, 1967) p. 38: '. . . par leur accord avec l'évolution économique et sociale, ils sont la grande force révolutionnaire qui produit l'avancement de l'individualisme.'

17 It is often noted that the other contemporary religious movement, partly a reaction to Evangelicalism, had equally strong connections with the Romantic Movement. This is true, and there can be no doubt that the Oxford Movement had its own part to play in affecting the development of Victorian culture. The Oxford Movement, however, cannot be thought of in the same way as Evangelicalism, as affecting the general sensibility at this time.

18 *Richard Chenevix Trench, Archbishop. Letters and Memorials*, ed. by the author of 'Charles Lowder' (1888) p. 53.

19 *Prelude* (text of 1805), ed. E. De Selincourt, revised ed. (1960) p. 235; XIII p. 209 ff.
20 *Essays and Tales By John Sterling*, ed. J. C. Hare (1858) II p. 504.
21 *Guesses at Truth By Two Brothers* (J. C. and A. W. Hare), 1st series, 4th ed. (1851) I p. 345. The first edition, the work of both brothers, appeared in 1827, but the elder, Augustus, died in 1834.
22 J. C. Hare, *The Victory of Faith and other Sermons* (1840) pp. 67–8.
23 *The Mission of the Comforter and other Sermons* (1846) I p. 263.
24 Ibid., p. 264.
25 *The Victory of Faith*, pp. 37–8.

Edward Bulwer Lytton

1 Lytton, *England and the English*, p. 111.
2 Ibid., pp. 112–13.
3 Ibid., p. 104.
4 Ibid., p. 97.
5 Ibid., p. 99.
6 Ibid., pp. 100–1.
7 'The Tale of a Dreamer', *Weeds and Wildflowers*, by E. G. L. B. (privately printed, 1826).
8 *Falkland* (1827), Pocket Volume Ed. (1888) p. 4.
9 Ibid., p. 5.
10 *Godolphin* (1833), Pocket Volume Ed. (1888) p. 239.
11 'The Critic – No. II. On Art in Fiction', *Monthly Chronicle*, I (1838) 139–40.
12 Ibid., p. 141.
13 *Pelham* (1828), Pocket Volume Ed. (1887) p. 170.
14 C. Kegan Paul, *William Godwin: His Friends and Contemporaries* (1876) II, pp. 304–6.
15 Pocket Volume Ed. (1887) p. xi.
16 'A Word to the Reader', *Ernest Maltravers* (1837).
17 *The Caxtons: A Family Picture* (1849) preface.

The Fiction of Harriet Martineau

1 'The Achievement of the Genius of Scott' (1832), *Miscellanies* (1836) I p. 52.
2 Ibid., p. 41.
3 Ibid., p. 52.
4 N. E. Rivensburg, *Harriet Martineau: An Example of Victorian Conflict* (1932) p. 21.
5 See *Letters of Thomas Carlyle to John Stuart Mill, John Sterling and Robert Brownell*, ed. A. Carlyle (1923) pp. 40–1.
6 The *Illustrations of Political Economy* appeared between 1832 and 1834. They were followed by *Poor Laws and Paupers Illustrated* (1833–4), the less successful *Illustrations of Taxation* (1834), and *Forest and Game Law Tales* (1845–6). An excellent account of their reception

and their background is provided in R. K. Webb's admirable book, *Harriet Martineau: A Radical Victorian* (1960).

7 *Harriet Martineau's Autobiography. With Memorials by Maria Weston Chapman*, 2nd ed. (1877) I p. 100.

8 'Miss Sedgwick's Works', *London and Westminster Review*, VI and XXVIII (1838) p. 46.

9 *Letters of Mary Shelley*, ed. P. L. Jones (1944) II p. 133.

10 *The Doctrine of Philosophical Necessity Illustrated; being an Appendix to the Disquisition relating to Matter and Spirit* (1792) p. 299.

11 *Deerbrook. A Novel* (1839) III p. 258.

12 Ibid., pp. 286–7.

13 T. Bosanquet, *Harriet Martineau* (1927) p. 126.

14 *Deerbrook*, III p. 276.

15 *Oliver Weld*, originally suggested by a reading of Thackeray's *Pendennis*, was to have been pseudonymously published by George Smith, through the agency of Charlotte Brontë. When they saw the manuscript of the first volume, both Smith and Brontë disapproved. The latter's priggish note (1 Jan 1852) to Martineau may be seen in *The Brontë's, Their Lives, Friendships, and Correspondence*, ed. C. Shorter and T. J. Wise (1932) III p. 303.

Frederick Denison Maurice

1 H. G. Wood, *Frederick Denison Maurice* (1950) p. 16.

2 *The Kingdom of Christ Or Hints to a Quaker Respecting the Principles, Constitution and Ordinances of the Catholic Church* (1838) ed. A. R. Vidler, based on 2nd ed. of 1842 (1858) I p. 158.

3 Ibid., pp. 158–9.

4 'On Books', *The Friendship of Books and Other Lectures* (1880) III pp. 86–7.

5 'Sketches of Contemporary Authors, no. ix. – Sir Walter Scott', *Athenaeum*, No. 14 (14 Mar 1828) p. 217.

6 Letter to Charles Kingsley, 25 Feb 1851; *The Life of F. D. Maurice, chiefly told in his own letters* (1884) I p. 59.

7 Dedication to *The Kingdom of Christ*, 2nd ed. (1842) p. xvii.

8 See Mill's essays, 'Bentham' (1838) and 'Coleridge' (1840); *Dissertations and Discussions* (1859-75).

9 20 Aug 1838; *The Life of F. D. Maurice*, I p. 251.

10 *Autobiography of Dean Merivale*, ed. J. A. Merivale (1899) p. 80.

11 *Eustace Conway* (1834) II p. 96.

12 Ibid., III p. 82.

13 John Sterling's *Arthur Coningsby* (1833) bears on very closely related problems to those discussed in that of his friend, Maurice. They drifted apart in later years, as Sterling became less and less orthodox in religious matters, but their deepest disagreements were always about means rather than ends. *Reginald Dalton* (1823) was in some ways the most interesting of Lockhart's novels, genuinely experi-

mental, though very incoherent. G. H. Lewes's novels – *Ranthorpe* (1847) and *Rose Blanche and Violet* (1848) – show the influence of Goethe, Balzac and George Sand, but still compare very interestingly with the earlier attempts of Maurice, Sterling and Lockhart to embody contemporary psychological and spiritual problems in the novel.

14   *The Kingdom of Christ* (1858) I p. 216.
15   Ibid., I p. 219.
16   Ibid., I p. 158.
17   Ibid., I p. 220.
18   Ibid., I p. 221.
19   Ibid., II p. 336.
20   Ibid.

Thomas Carlyle

1   'Thomas Carlyle'; *Leader*, VI (27 Oct 1855) 1034–5; *Essays of George Eliot*, ed. T. Pinney (1968) pp. 213–14.
2   'On the State of German Literature' (1827), *Critical and Miscellaneous Essays*, ed. H. D. Traill (1905) I p. 83.
3   'Burns' (1828), *Essays*, I p. 272.
4   'On the State of German Literature' (1827), *Essays*, I p. 51.
5   Ibid., p. 52.
6   28 Oct 1822, *Collected Letters of Thomas and Jane Welsh Carlyle*, ed. C. R. Saunders *et al.* (1970) II pp. 188–9.
7   16 Dec 1822, ibid., pp. 229–30.
8   For the text of 'Illudo Chartis' see M. P. King, ' "Illudo Chartis" : An Initial Study in Carlyle's Mode of Composition', *Modern Language Review*, XLIX (1954).
9   *Last Words of Thomas Carlyle* (1892) pp. 23–4.
10   Ibid., p. 36.
11   Ibid., p. 98.
12   *Sartor Resartus* (1833–4), book 1, chapter x.
13   'On Biography' (1832), *Essays*, III p. 55.
14   Ibid., p. 56.
15   Ibid., p. 57.
16   'Diderot' (1833), *Essays*, III p. 178.
17   Ibid.
18   'On the State of German Literature' (1827), *Essays*, I p. 66.
19   'Carlyle', *Leader*, VI, 1034–5; *Essays of George Eliot*, p. 215.
20   *London and Westminster Review*, XXVII (July 1837) 17–53; *Thomas Carlyle, the Critical Heritage*, ed. J. P. Seigel (1971) p. 54.

PART III   THE DEVELOPMENT OF REALIST FICTION

1   John Morley, *The Life of Richard Cobden* (1879; popular ed., 1903) pp. 89–90.
2   Benjamin Disraeli (1804–81), produced his first novel – *Vivian Grey* –

in 1826–7. At intervals until his death he produced a further thirteen works of fiction.

3 See W. F. Monypenny and G. E. Buckle, *The Life of Benjamin Disraeli, Earl of Beaconsfield* (1910-1920; new ed., 1929) p. 196.

4 *Morning Chronicle*, 13 May 1845; *William Makepeace Thackeray's Contributions to the Morning Chronicle*, ed. G. N. Ray (1955) p. 82.

5 'Three Novels', *Westminster Review*, LXVI (Oct 1856) 571–8; *Essays of George Eliot*, ed. Pinney, p. 329.

6 *Modern Painters*, II (1846), Part III, section I, chapter 2.

7 Ibid., chapter 12.

8 Ibid.

9 Ibid., III (1856), Part IV, chapter 7.

10 Ibid.

11 Ibid., II (1846) Part III, section I, chapter 14.

12 'German Wit: Heinrich Heine,' *Westminster Review*, LXV (Jan 1856) 1–33; *Essays of George Eliot*, p. 219.

13 *Critical and Miscellaneous Essays*, ed. Traill, I p. 17.

14 G. H. Ford, *Dickens and His Readers* (1955; 1965 ed.) p. 155.

15 D. Masson, *British Novelists and Their Styles* (1859; repr. 1969) p. 248.

16 John Forster, *The Life of Charles Dickens* (1872–4) VII, chapter 1.

17 John Forster, review of *Henry Esmond*, *Examiner* (13 Nov 1852) 723–6; *Thackeray, the Critical Heritage*, ed. G. Tillotson and D. Hawes, p. 148.

18 'The Storm-Cloud of the Nineteenth Century' (1884), *Thackeray, the Critical Heritage*, p. 87.

19 11 Jan 1857, *Letters of George Eliot*, ed. G. Haight (1954) II p. 348.

20 4 Jan 1858 (apropos of *The Virginians*), *Letters of George Meredith*, ed. C. L. Cline (1970) I p. 31.

21 19 Dec 1849, 11 Dec 1847 and 18 Oct 1848, *The Brontë Life and Letters*, ed. C. Shorter (1908) II pp. 101, 373, 459.

22 *Letters and Private Papers of William Makepeace Thackeray*, ed. G. N. Ray (1946) II p. 691.

23 'Charity and Humour' (1852), *Works of William Makepeace Thackeray*, Biographical Ed. (1898) VII p. 725.

24 *The Book of Snobs* (1848), *Works*, VI p. 464.

25 R. Bell, *Fraser's Magazine* (Sep 1848) 320–3; *Letters and Private Papers*, II p. 423.

26 3 Sep 1848, *Letters and Private Papers*, II pp. 423–4.

27 J. Forster, *Examiner* (22 July 1848) p. 468.

28 *Letters and Private Papers*, II p. 424.

29 Ibid. The italics are mine.

30 'On Carlyle' (1839); *Essays and Tales by John Sterling*, ed. Hare, pp. 376–7.

31 Ibid.

32 Ibid., p. 327.

33 Ibid., p. 326.
34 G. H. Lewes, *The Apprenticeship of Life; Leader* (6 Apr 1850) 43.
35 'Realism in Art: Recent German Fiction', *Westminster Review*, LXX (Oct 1858) 494.
36 Ibid., p. 493.

The Realism of Dickens

1 *Dombey and Son* (1847–8) chapter XL.
2 'Ginshops', *Sketches by Boz* (1836–7).
3 *Oliver Twist* (1837–8) chapter L.
4 *Dombey and Son*, chapter XX.
5 Ibid., chapter LV.
6 Ibid.
7 Ibid.
8 *Great Expectations* (1860–1) chapter LVI.
9 Ibid., chapter 1.
10 Ibid., chapter XXLII.
11 Ibid., chapter I.
12 Ibid., chapter II.

The History of Henry Esmond

1 *An Autobiography* (1883), ed. F. Page (1950) pp. 41 and 186.
2 *Harriet Martineau's Autobiography*, II p. 376.
3 *The History of Henry Esmond* (1852), *Works of William Makepeace Thackeray*, VII, pp. 418–19.
4 Ibid., p. 15.
5 Ibid., p. 109.
6 Ibid., p. 157.
7 Ibid., p. 192.
8 Ibid., p. 195.
9 Ibid., p. 202.
10 Ibid., p. 302.
11 Ibid., p. 334.
12 Ibid., p. 419.

George Eliot

1 O. Elton, *A Survey of English Literature, 1830–1880* (1920); *A Century of George Eliot Criticism*, ed. G. Haight (1965) p. 190.
2 E. S. Dallas, *The Times* (12 Apr 1859); *A Century of George Eliot Criticism*, p. 3.
3 'The Influence of Rationalism,' *Fortnightly Review*, I (15 May 1865); *Essays of George Eliot*, p. 413.
4 'The Progress of the Intellect', *Westminster Review*, LIV (Jan 1851); *Essays of George Eliot*, p. 31.

5   'The Natural History of German Life', *Westminster Review*, LXVI (July 1856); *Essays of George Eliot*, p. 271.
6   Ibid., pp. 271–2.
7   'The Sad Fortunes of the Rev. Amos Barton', chapter V.
8   *Adam Bede* (1859) chapter XVII.
9   *The Mill on the Floss* (1860), 'The Valley of Humiliation', chapter I.
10 Ibid., chapter III.
11 'The Novels of George Eliot', *Atlantic Monthly*, 18 (Oct 1860) 479–92; *A Century of George Eliot Criticism*, p. 52.
12 *The Mill on the Floss*, 'Boy and Girl', chapter XII.

George Meredith

1   H. G. Wells, *The New Machiavelli* (1911), 'Adolescence', p. 7; *George Meredith, the Critical Heritage*, ed. I. Williams (1971) pp. 518–19.
2   P. Lubbock, *Quarterly Review*, CCXVI (Apr 1910); *George Meredith, the Critical Heritage*, p. 518.
3   S. P. Sherman, *Nation*, LXXXVIII (3 June 1909); *George Meredith, the Critical Heritage*, pp. 491–2.
4   J. B. Priestley, *George Meredith* (1926) p. 67.
5   See M. B. Forman, *George Meredith and the Monthly Observer*.
6   Quoted by E. Clodd, 'George Meredith: Some Recollections', *Fortnightly Review* (July 1909) 18–31.
7   On the Idea of Comedy . . . (1877); *Works of George Meredith*, XXXII (1898) p. 15.
8   Ibid., p. 65.
9   *Letters of George Meredith*, ed. C. L. Cline (1970) I p. 161.
10 *Westminster Review*, XII (Oct 1857) 600.
11 *Westminster Review*, XI (Apr 1857) 608.
12 *Works*, XVII p. 19.
13 Ibid., p. 23.
14 Ibid.
15 Meredith recognised this himself quite soon after the novel was published and put it through two stages of revision, cutting out most of the first three chapters for the Tauchnitz edition of 1878 and another whole chapter after the Macmillan edition of 1896. The excised material is given in *Works* (1911) XXXVI.
16 *Letters*, I 485.
17 *Works*, XIII p. 7.
18 E. M. Forster, *Aspects of the Novel* (1927; repr. 1963), 99.
19 *Works*, XIII pp. 354–5.
20 Ibid., p. 337.

CONCLUSION

1   *Portrait of a Lady* (1881; New York ed., 1908) II p. 435.

Index of Names and Titles

218   Index of Names and Titles

220   *Index of Names and Titles*

Wells, H. G., 184, 201
Welsh, A., 30
Welsh, J., 100, 101
Werther, 8, 47
Wilhelm Meister, 23, 24, 71, 100, 102
Wood, H. G., 85
Wooton Reinfred, 102–5, 106

Wordsworth, W., 11, 47, 50, 54, 55, 56, 64, 65, 86, 87, 89, 97, 98, 171

Yeats, W. B., 186

Zanoni, 73
Zeluco, 70